A CATALAN COOKERY BOOK

IRVING DAVIS (1889–1967) was an antiquarian book dealer, bibliophile and cook whose life forms a glorious coda to that love affair with the Mediterranean and its civilization that has long held the English, and other north-Europeans, in its thrall. His first bookshop was in Florence, where he was in partnership with Giuseppe Orioli from 1911. This book which celebrates the cookery of Catalonia is his most permanent and appealing epitaph, though for bibliographers there are 170 exemplary catalogues of early printed books.

A Catalan Cookery Book was privately published a few years after his death, but this new edition is the first time it has been generally available. It is a fragment of a longer projected work but Irving Davis was a man who sought perfection and he did not live to complete it. Yet there is enough here for us to enjoy and to cook from. The direct exuberance of Catalan cookery is captured in these pages. The recipes are not 'impossible' – even if they seemed to be to a man who was writing in the days (the '50s) when peppers and chiles were a rarity and tomatoes invariably from greenhouses in Holland.

The book is topped and tailed by the author Patience Gray who knew Irving Davis well. Her own book, *Honey from a Weed* celebrates inimitably the Mediterranean, its food and its culture, and may be said to form part of the same culinary and intellectual tradition.

A CATALAN COOKERY BOOK

Irving Davis (1889–1967)

A CATALAN COOKERY BOOK

A Collection of Impossible Recipes

by

IRVING DAVIS

Edited by Patience Gray.
With eleven engravings by Nicole.

PROSPECT BOOKS
1999

First published in this form in 1999 by Prospect Books,
Allaleigh House, Blackawton, Totnes, Devon TQ9 7DL.

British Library Cataloguing in Publication Data:
A CIP record for this book is available from the British Library.

The cover to the Prospect Books edition was designed and drawn by Corinna Sargood.

ISBN 0 907325 92 0

Printed and bound by the Cromwell Press, Trowbridge, Wiltshire.

CONTENTS

Publisher's note

This book was first published privately in an edition of 165 copies commissioned by Lucien Scheler in September 1969, printed at the Imprimerie Union and the Atelier Leblanc, Paris.

The present edition, although of slightly smaller format, has attempted to reproduce the typography and design of the original. However, there are compromises stemming from the use of electronic typesetting, offset printing and photographic reproduction of the engravings: inevitable consequences of the decision to produce a trade version of this book. However, undertaking the work anew has permitted the addition of some material relating to Irving Davis: the obituary by his friend Lucien Scheler, the text of a fragment of autobiography by Davis himself, and a memory by Patience Gray, written after his death.

The publisher is grateful to Ianthe Carswell, Patience Gray, Nicole Fenosa and Lucien Scheler for their collaboration in bringing this commercial edition to fruition, thus allowing a wider public to appreciate the life of Irving Davis.

INTRODUCTION

The author of this Catalan Cookery Book was ruled by passion, a passion for truth. No need, therefore, to question the authenticity of these recipes. Irving Davis was a *connaisseur* of priceless manuscripts and early printed books, he was a gourmet and a marvellous cook.

Irving's book catalogues had a poetic quality which emanated partly from the precision with which he described his treasures. He set as rigorous a standard of veracity in culinary matters as he practised in cataloguing books.

Today, when we seem to be participating in a new Victorian Age reflected in cooking by the emphasis placed on gargantuan repasts recommended in enormous tomes stuffed with spectacular colour photographs, the *classical* conception of cooking has all but vanished. At Irving's table, one could still experience its full poetic meaning. The meals he made reflected the diametrically opposite conjunction of liberality and frugality, which, characterizing his way of life, has always been the secret of culinary achievement. Here the mechanics of creation —forethought, selection, trouble, timing— were erased by the disarming simplicity of the outcome, which gave rise only to pleasure and delight. Irving's dishes were an invocation to the ideal; his method of presenting them celebrated his Mediterranean past.

It was the frugality of the Catalan culinary tradition combined with the matchless quality of the materials employed which first inspired him to begin this book, the distilled delight of several summers spent at Vendrell with his friends, the Catalan sculptor Apel.les Fenosa and his wife Nicole.

There is an extremity in the climate there reflected in violent physical transitions, where fasting —actual physical privation arising from exposure to the hallucinatory effects of heat, dust, light— gives place not to just eating, but to feasting. In such conditions a handful of tomatoes, a plate of grilled sardines, some rustic bread and a trickle of wine suddenly take on the aspect of a feast, fit not only for man but for the Gods.

Being above all a perfectionist, Irving was naturally informed with pessimism, which inspired the subtitle of this culinary fragment: *A Collection of Impossible Recipes.* Impossible they seemed to him to achieve in another climate, with less than perfect materials, without the patience and the skill, (two requirements relating to chopping and grinding which transform what at first sight appear to be inordinately simple recipes) and, above all, without the golden Catalan wine whose very strength and fire demand that it be poured into the mouth in a thin stream from the reluctant spout of the *porró,* wine poured like an invocation, and which, passed from hand to hand, turns the humblest dish into a cause for celebration.

I have had the singular privilege of editing this uncompleted manuscript and in the course of doing so, have found it practicable to make a number of the dishes here described whose delicacy and flavour are without parallel even when made in a London kitchen. I have taken the liberty of writing the notes on cooking procedure which Irving always intended to include and which he discussed with me. But this little book is not so much a collection of culinary admonitions as the distilled essence of a fast vanishing way of life.

PATIENCE GRAY

February 1968

PREFACE

I have tried to write a book of Catalan cookery, selecting from the many the most typical dishes, some of which I have cooked and others which I hope to cook one day. Catalonia is a little individual island in the vast Spanish sea. It was only finally included in the Kingdom of Spain at the beginning of the 16th century. The Catalans are a proud and perhaps, compared to the majority of Mediterraneans, a silent people, nursing their grievances, their language and their culinary traditions.

Before all these traditional dishes disappear into as remote a past as those of Taille-vent and before the waves of tourists have swamped Catalonia and its beaches, it seems to me worth while to try and record some of them.

Besides the original inhabitants of this section of the Iberian peninsula there have been the Phoenicians, the Greeks, the Romans and the Moors. I am convinced that all these temporary "visitors" have left traces of their cooking.

Perhaps the most startling and unusual quality of Catalan cookery is the mixture of sweet ingredients with chicken, rabbit and sometimes other meat dishes; see the recipe for rabbit with prunes, rabbit with chocolate and snails, in the body of the book. Such dishes must surely be remnants of the days before the introduction of the tomato. It was the Spaniards who discovered the beneficent effects of chocolate in Mexico at the beginning of the 16th century and brought the cocoa bean to Europe. And it was they who likewise brought the tomato from Peru at the end of that century. The tomato of course, as in most Mediterranean countries, is all conquering and it is difficult to think how the southern Latins cooked before this all powerful vegetable invaded Europe. The basis of Italian cookery, as is well known, is the *soffritto,* that is onions, herbs simmered in oil with tomatoes —in Catalonia, with some variations, the *sofregit.* But this is usually associated with the *picada,* a mixture of pounded almonds, pine-kernels, garlic and parsley, also with variations described overleaf.

I have called the work a *Catalan Cookery Book* with a subtitle *A Collection of Impossible Recipes,* impossible for the most part to execute in England. The most you can do is to try to adapt them. Nothing is to me more annoying than to read some of the numerous cookery books which pretend to be practical and which gaily tell you to take certain ingredients which you would have to go to the ends of the earth to find. Why not treat a cookery book as an entertainment as interesting to read as a detective story or a substitute for radio or television at night?

IRVING DAVIS

A NOTE ON COOKING PROCEDURES

Probably the most distinctive characteristic of Catalan cookery is the sofregit, *the initial sauce usually consisting of onions, though sometimes garlic, and tomatoes in which fish, meat, beans are slowly cooked. Its excellence depends upon the degree of fineness with which the onions are chopped and their subsequent immersion in hot olive oil* (sofregit *means under-fried) for long enough to acquire a golden colour and then, combining with the peeled and crushed tomatoes, to eventually disappear into a homogeneous sauce. It should here be said that the Spanish onion is notable for its size and mildness compared with English ones. The tomatoes too are of another species, much larger, firmer and of more delicious flavour. Perfectly ripe tomatoes are only used in cooking, unripe green tomatoes with the merest flush are used in salads. This has something to do with the rate at which everything in that climate decays; marketing is done every day.*

The sofregit, *as will be seen from the following pages, is often associated with the* picada, *the* coup de bec *or peck which, added towards the end of the cooking, gives a particular piquancy to a dish. This normally consists of garlic, peeled almonds, sometimes pine-kernels, chopped parsley, pounded in that order very finely in a mortar, with on special occasions various additions which include items such as ground black pepper, hazel-nuts, hot chilli peppers, pimentos first roasted in the ashes of a woodfire, and sometimes chocolate and dry biscuits* (carquinyolis) *finely ground in the mortar for the purpose of flavouring or thickening a sauce. Speed in Catalan cooking is associated largely with frying, (see recipes for* Llomillo arrebossat, *pork fried in a coating of bread-crumbs,* truites *which are omelettes, and fried vegetables such as* albergínies *and* mongetes— *i.e. aubergines and beans). Fresh fish is also cooked at speed in a prepared* court-bouillon *as are such delicately flavoured sea food as mussels which tend to toughen if cooking is prolonged*

Slow cooking in earthenware vessels which have been from time immemorial fired by charcoal is more frequent. The essential quality of such dishes can often be retained by cooking them in earthenware pots in a slow oven instead of on top of the modern gas or electric stove. An enamelled cocotte en fonte, *iron pot with a lid, is another solution for the slow cooking of partridges, rabbit, chicken.*

In many instances the earthenware olla *has been replaced by tall aluminium lidded saucepans similar to the French* marmite *which was of course originally of earthenware, now that the source of heat derives more often from calor gas than the traditional charcoal.*

The size of the paella, *a shallow iron pan with two handles, is far more capacious than any English frying pan and it is difficult to make a* paella *without it, its dimensions relating to the evaporation of the sauce which determines the perfect cooking of the rice, which at a given moment is both cooked and dry (i.e. all the liquid that has not been absorbed by the rice has evaporated).*

The frequent reference to woodfires on the glowing embers of which, closely tended and fanned, fish are grilled and vegetables—aubergines, pimentos, onions, tomatoes— (see Escalivada), *are roasted in Catalonia is simply normal practice, many households having a raised hearth in the yard on which is burnt the pungent and aromatic scrub of the* maquis. *It is the special nature of the wood burned which contributes its flavour to grilled food, combined with the aromatic plants, rosemary and thyme, which are cast on the embers at the moment of grilling.*

P. G.

SOUPS

ESCUDELLA DE CARBASSA I MONGETES BLANQUES
Pumpkin and Haricot Bean Soup

SOPA DE FARIGOLA
Thyme Soup

SOPA DE MONGETES
Bean Soup

SOPA DE RAP
Potage de baudroie

ESCUDELLA DE CARBASSA
I MONGETES BLANQUES

Pumpkin and Haricot Bean Soup

1 lb of pumpkin, ¹/₂ lb of haricot beans,
¹/₂ lb of lean shoulder of salt pork,
a ham bone, 1 botifarra negra *(blood sausage),*
a small piece of fat unsmoked pork (llard ranci),
a few bay leaves, an onion, a handful of rice per person.

Soak the beans the night before. In a large pot put three pints of water, the beans, the bay leaves, the ham bone, the shoulder of pork and the blood sausage. Bring to the boil, skim, and boil for twenty minutes. Then add the pumpkin cut into small pieces, the onion chopped, the 'rancid pork' well floured. Continue to boil slowly until the beans and the pumpkin are very thoroughly cooked. This will take about an hour and a half.

Then add the rice which should cook for about twenty minutes.

This soup should neither be too thick nor too thin.

I prepared this soup myself for twelve people and of course increased the quantity of ingredients. Can one get 'rancid lard' in England? I fancy not. This is an old piece of pork which has a bitter taste, only a very small piece is used. The pumpkin which I used was quite different from English pumpkins. The skin was yellowish blue and had a rocky formation.

SOPA DE FARIGOLA
Thyme Soup

1 1/2 pints of water,
slices of stale bread,
a branch of dried thyme,
olive oil, salt.

In a saucepan boil the water and when boiling put in the thyme. While the water is boiling put the slices of bread very finely cut in each plate, salt the slices of bread and pour olive oil on them. Do not be stingy with the oil. If you think this is not enough you can break a very fresh egg in each plate. When the thyme has infused for two or three minutes, pour the water —gently if you have put an egg— into each soup-plate.

This is the simplest of soups eaten mainly by shepherds, but very useful as a cure for a hangover.

SOPA DE MONGETES
Bean Soup

1 ¹/₂ lb of red beans,
four medium-sized potatoes peeled,
a very ripe tomato cut into pieces,
one clove of garlic not peeled, which
you crush with your fist,
half a soup-spoon of red pimento,
an onion finely hashed, salt to taste.

Put the beans in a sufficient quantity of cold water and cook them for half an hour. Drain them and add twice the quantity of water to their volume. When they have cooked for about an hour and are tender, add all the other ingredients. Cook for a further half hour. You can if you wish add a little cut up bacon. Senyor Bonet added some slices of *sobressada*, but you are unlikely to find this kind of smoked sausage in England.

If the red beans employed in this dish are not freshly husked they will need a preliminary soaking the day before, in water with a pinch of bicarbonate.

Recipe given to me by Senyor Juan Bonet Ribas of Cala Saladas

SOPA DE RAP
Potage de Baudroie

The head of this fish,
one onion, one tomato, a large
slice of bread per head, finely cut,
olive oil.

Clean the head of the fish and put it in a pan in cold water. Chop the onion finely, brown it in oil and put in the cut up tomato. Cook gently for half an hour. Put this preparation into the fish-pan, bring to the boil and boil for ten minutes.

Strain the contents of the saucepan, keeping the broth.

Remove the skin from the head of the fish and cut up any of the flesh that adheres to it into small pieces. Pass this and what remains in the strainer through a *moulinette* and put it into the broth. Add the bread and boil for five minutes, stirring all the time with an egg whisk.

See *Rap a la marinera* for what to do with the body of the fish.

OMELETTES

TRUITA D'ALBERGÍNIA
Aubergine Omelette

TRUITA DE CARXOFA
Artichoke Omelette

TRUITA D'ESPÀRRECS DEL BOSC
Wild Asparagus Omelette

TRUITA DE MONGETES
Haricot Bean Omelette

TRUITA AMB TRAMPA
Trick Omelette

TRUITES
Omelettes

It is impossible to enumerate all the different kinds of omelettes eaten in Catalonia. You can put almost anything you like in one except perhaps fish, with the exception of those called *xanguet* which is whitebait. The method of making them is always the same.

TRUITA D'ALBERGÍNIA
Aubergine Omelette

Cut the aubergine into fairly thick slices without peeling. Salt lightly and leave for about an hour to remove the superfluous water. Dry well and throw into hot oil. Beat the eggs and throw them onto the aubergine slices. Stir a little and fold as a normal omelette.

TRUITA DE CARXOFA
Artichoke Omelette

For this dish you need small artichokes which are grown in Spain and Italy, not the green monsters imported from France. Remove the hard outer leaves. Cut off the prickly points of the leaves and cut what remains into small vertical strips. Throw into hot oil, and proceed as above.

TRUITA D'ESPARRECS DEL BOSC
Wild Asparagus Omelette

Gather some wild asparagus (which certainly do not grow in England as far as I know). Clean and fry in hot oil for a few minutes. Proceed as above.

TRUITA DE MONGETES
Haricot Bean Omelette

As everyone knows, haricot beans are soaked the night before and cooked slowly for about an hour and a half. If you have any left over use them for an omelette. Throw into the pan for a few minutes with very hot oil and proceed as above.

TRUITA AMB TRAMPA
Trick Omelette

For 2 people, a large slice of bread from which the crust has
been removed, 3 eggs, an onion, a tomato,
1/2 a coffee-spoonful of red pepper,
a soup-spoonful of flour,
a handful of shelled green peas,
a little parsley.

Soak the slice of bread in water, then remove it and squeeze it thoroughly with your hand. Break the three eggs in a dish and beat, add the bread, season and mix well. Throw the mixture into hot oil. Fry on both sides and keep in a warm dish. Have ready a *sofregit* consisting of an onion finely chopped which has been well browned in a frying pan, and to which you have added the peeled tomato and red pepper. This should cook for about twenty minutes until the water from the tomato has evaporated. Sprinkle the *sofregit* with flour and stir so that it does not stick.

Cut the omelette in four and put it into the pan in this sauce, adding just enough hot water to cover. Put in the peas already cooked and the chopped parsley. Cover and simmer for a quarter of an hour.

PASTA

MACARRONS AL FORN
Macaroni in the oven

MACARRONS AL FORN
Macaroni in the oven

1 ½ lb of macaroni, an onion, two chicken livers,
the blood of a chicken, two very ripe tomatoes,
oil, 2 ounces of grated Gruyere cheese.

Boil the macaroni, drain it, rinse in cold water, drain thoroughly. In the meantime brown the onion finely chopped, add the chicken livers finely cut and the chicken's blood. Cook for a few minutes and then add the peeled tomatoes. Cook this for a quarter of an hour. Put the macaroni in a well-oiled dish which goes into the oven. Pour the sauce over it, sprinkle it with cheese, and put in a hot oven until the cheese browns.

Shades of pasta-eaters from Turin to Sicily! What would they think of this dish, probably turn in their graves! But I have already said that everything is different in Catalonia. Unless you care for cutting chicken's throats, or have a friend who does, I do not think you will find this curdled blood in England. Yet it is sold in the market at Vendrell.

Recipe given to me by Anita Simal Llonch

SNAILS

CARGOLS
Snails

CARGOLS DOLÇOS I PICANTS
Snails in sweet and piquant sauce

CARGOLS
Snails

This is a recipe for cooking snails, but first I must explain how to clean them. There are a good many different kinds of snails, some of which are considered better than others in Catalonia. Among the best are the *vaques* and the *cristians*! The *vaques* are usually found near trees in sunshine after rain; the *cristians* are usually found in vineyards. First starve your snails. Then put them in a bucket of cold water, rub them vigorously against each other with your hands, throw away the water and put them in a very little water with a large handful of salt and rub as above for ten minutes. Next, throw them into cold water and change the water six or seven times until they do not froth any more.

Then put them in a pan in cold water with thyme and bay leaves and cook uncovered very slowly, but be careful that the snails do not crawl over the sides while the water is heating. When the water boils, salt and cook gently for an hour. Drain them and keep some of the water in which they have cooked.

CARGOLS DOLÇOS I PICANTS
Snails in sweet and piquant sauce

2 lbs of snails for four persons,
2 onions, 4 tomatoes,
a coffee-spoonful of sugar, a pinch of flour,
a segment of hot red chilli pepper.

Grate the onions, put them in hot oil in a pan and brown them, add the four peeled tomatoes crushed. Cook slowly. Put in the sugar and the flour and the chilli pepper cut very fine. Stir, then add slowly some of the water in which the snails have cooked. When this has reduced, add a little more of the water. Repeat this operation several times, say for twenty minutes. Now at last put the snails into this sauce and cook for fifteen minutes continually stirring. You can eat this dish hot or cold.

I suppose there are some snails in England but probably of a less noble race than those named above. In any case if you collect them you will reap a double advantage, first of all your flowers will not be devoured and secondly you will have an economical dinner.

SEA FOOD

Introduction: Four ways of cooking fish

ARENGADES
Salt herrings grilled; grilled, with *pa amb tomàquet*;
uncooked, with *palates i mongetes*

ARENGADES AMB CASACA
Salt herrings fried in batter

ARENGADA AMB OU FERRAT
Salt herring with fried eggs

BACALLÀ
Salt cod

BACALLÀ AMB PANSES I PINYONS
Salt cod with raisins and pine-kernels

BACALLÀ ESQUEIXAT
Flaked salt cod

BACALLÀ A LA LLAUNA
Salt cod cooked in an oven dish

CIGRONS, ESPINACS, OUS I BACALLÀ
Chick-peas, spinach, eggs and salt cod

BARAT
Mackerel

CALAMARS
Squid

CALDERETA
A kind of paella made in an earthenware pot:
a dish of rock fishes, followed by a dish of rice

LLAGOSTA A LA CATALANA
Langouste à la catalane

MUSCLOS
Mussels

RAP A LA MARINERA
Baudroie à la marinière

ROMESCO I
A piquant sauce for grey mullet, sea bream, sea bass, cod, etc.

ROMESCO II
A hotter version for grilled fish

SARDINES EN ESCABETX
Marinated sardines

SARSUELA
A variety of fish and shellfish
cooked in a highly spiced sauce

PAELLA

SEA FOOD

As most of Catalonia is either, like the Costa Brava, by the seaside or at any rate within easy reach of the sea, it is not surprising that the main food is sea food. Anyone who has spent three summers as I have in Vendrell and been every morning to the market will be amazed at the quantity and variety of fish, many of which have no English name. They will be equally surprised at the high price. Of course there are exceptions, for instance sardines and mackerel. English visitors will also for the most part be unfamiliar with the flavour of fresh fish, which very few people have the luck to eat in England.

There are four main ways of cooking fish:

FRYING

Clean, wash and dry the fish thoroughly, flour it, put it into a pan of boiling oil (which must be olive oil, not lard or any other substitute), brown on one side, then on the other, and drain it.

GRILLING

Another way of cooking any fish is to prepare it first as in the recipe for *barat* (mackerel) and then grill it. A very large fish, such as *tuna,* should be cut into slices. The fish, large or small, is cooked on the embers of a woodfire, placing it on a grill. Fish cooked in this way, like many Catalan dishes, is served with olive oil.

IN THE OVEN

Cook in an oven dish. Generally large white-fleshed fish such as bream, grey mullet and sea bass are used. Clean and scale the fish, cut it as far as the centre bone in even slices, in each put a slice of lemon. Make a hash of one or two onions, two peeled and crushed tomatoes, add some chopped parsley, a little red paprika pepper and naturally salt. Moisten the fish generously with olive oil, and cover with this sauce. Put in a moderate oven and after fifteen minutes add a glass of dry white wine, cook for another half hour basting often.

PEIX A LA PLANXA

Another popular way of cooking fish is directly on top of the range on which you have put a few drops of oil to prevent burning. This can easily be done in England by those who have an Aga stove.

ARENGADES
Salt herrings

Arengada is a dried and salted herring. It is the cheapest food that exists in Spain. In fact they only cost one peseta each this year (1964).

There are several ways of eating them, perhaps the most delicious is to grill them a moment on each side. Then put them on a slice of bread, cut off the head, remove the central bone. Soak the bread with olive oil. Don't be mean with the oil. This is always eaten with a bunch of muscat grapes. It corresponds to the Italian *prosciutto con melone,* perhaps a little less delicate. It is sure to give you a thirst, perhaps not a defect, so drink plenty of white wine with it.

A refinement on this typical Catalan supper dish is to eat the *arengada* with *pa amb tomàquet* (see recipe).

Another way of eating this salt herring is simply to clean it and eat it uncooked with *patates i mongetes* for which I also give the recipe. A cheap supper.

ARENGADES AMB CASACA
Salt herrings fried in batter

For four dried and salted herrings, one egg and a cup of flour. The day before cooking, soak the *arengades,* next day remove the heads and clean. Beat up the whole egg with the flour, making a thick paste. Dip the *arengades* in this paste until they are well coated. Throw them into a pan of boiling oil.

ARENGADA AMB OU FERRAT
Salt herring with fried eggs

Heat some oil in a pan, fry your egg, put it on your plate and in the same pan fry the herring cleaned or uncleaned as you prefer.

And these are two more cheap and nourishing suppers.

BACALLÀ AMB PANSES I PINYONS
Salt cod with raisins and pine-kernels

1 lb of salt cod or two pieces per person,
well soaked in water to remove the salt,
3 onions, 4 ounces of pine-kernels and a generous handful of raisins.

Dry the salt cod, flour it and fry lightly in a little oil, then remove from the pan. Fry the onions cut in slices. When these are browned put the cod back in the pan at the same time as the pine-kernels which must first be pounded in a mortar, reduced to a powder, and then diluted with a little water. Add the raisins and cook without a lid for thirty minutes.

BACALLÀ ESQUEIXAT
Flaked salt cod

One pound approximately of salt cod. Choose a thick piece. Skin and flake with your fingers, being careful to remove any bones or fibres, an easier operation than it sounds. Soak for one hour in water. Rinse well and press out all the water. Put the flaked cod in a dish and add plenty of olive oil, chopped garlic and parsley.

Salt cod is extremely appreciated in the Mediterranean, I cannot think why. Prepared in this fashion it is eaten cold as an *hors-d'œuvre*.

BACALLÀ A LA LLAUNA
Salt cod cooked in an oven dish

2 lbs of bacallà, *(2 pieces for each person),*
5 cloves of garlic, 2 lbs of ripe tomatoes,
2 extra cloves of garlic, parsley.
These quantities will serve four people.

Soak the pieces of cod the day before. The next day rinse them well, dry in a cloth and fry in olive oil about five minutes on each side, having first lightly dusted them with flour. Remove the fish from the pan. Chop the five cloves of garlic finely, brown them in the same pan, add the tomatoes peeled, and crush them in the pan. Cook until the sauce is reduced.

Take a shallow dish called in Catalan *llauna*. Place the pieces of salt cod in it, cover with the sauce and cook uncovered in a moderate oven for half an hour.

Before serving sprinkle the dish with two cloves of fresh garlic finely chopped with a handful of parsley.

CIGRONS, ESPINACS, OUS I BACALLÀ
Chick-peas, spinach, eggs and salt cod

2 lbs of spinach, 1 lb of chick-peas,
one hard-boiled egg per person,
4 fairly large pieces of bacallà *(about 1 lb),*
4 cloves of garlic, oil and salt.

Wash the spinach, drain it, and rub it in your hands with salt. Put some oil in a pan, heat it and throw in the garlic finely cut. When it is just browned put in the spinach and cook on a low flame for ten minutes, stirring. Now add the chick-peas which must be cooked in advance (*i.e.* soaked overnight and simmered for four hours), with a little of the water in which they have cooked. Continue cooking for fifteen minutes. Then add the salt cod floured and fried separately, and at the same time the hard-boiled eggs cut into slices, all this a minute or two before serving.

BARAT
Mackerel

1 large or 2 small mackerels,
salt, parsley, garlic, pepper,
powdered sweet pimento, a lemon.

Clean and split the mackerel, cut off the head and carefully remove the backbone. Cut the parsley and chop half a clove of garlic for each fish, add salt and pepper, a pinch of powdered sweet pimento and a few drops of lemon juice, and anoint the fish with this.

The fish should be prepared two hours before grilling them on a woodfire. The fish prepared in this way can also be cooked in the oven, but first oil the dish.

CALAMARS
Squid

2 lbs of squid,
flour, soda water.

Wash the squid, remove what is inside (the transparent cartilage and ink-bag), also the fine skin which covers it.

Cut the squid into rings and moisten them with a jet of soda water from a siphon. Roll the rings in flour and throw them into very hot olive oil.

CALDERETA

A kind of *paella* made in an earthenware pot:
a dish of rock fishes followed by a dish of rice

Caldereta means cauldron. This is a dish of rock fishes and rice cooked in the same *sofregit* in one vessel, normally earthenware.

5 rockfishes per head chosen from rascassa, donzella, sara, esparrall, calamar (squid),
1 small cup of rice per person and 3 times the quantity of water, (it is very important
that the volume of water should be 3 times that of the rice employed),
1 head of garlic, 2 large very ripe tomatoes,
1/2 a soup-spoonful of powdered pimento, 2 pinches of saffron.

To prepare the *sofregit* put four to eight large spoonfuls of oil in the paella. Now use your fist on the head of garlic to separate the cloves, and use it again to crush each one of them. Heat the oil and brown the crushed garlic, add the tomatoes already peeled and cut into small pieces, cook very gently for at least half an hour. Then add the powdered pimento and the saffron.

Stir the calculated quantity of water into this preparation and transfer to an upright earthenware pot called an *olla*. Put the cleaned fish in the *olla*, increase the heat and cook for ten minutes after the liquor boils. Remove the fish onto a plate and keep them warm. Put in the rice, unwashed, and cook for twenty minutes. Let it stand for five minutes before serving. The fish is eaten before the rice.

It is most improbable that you will find either an *olla* or any of the fish which I have mentioned, so perhaps you had just better read about this dish and wait till you come to Catalonia to eat it. You could of course try to substitute some of our large white fish cut into slices and small red mullets would be useful, but do not use any oily fish such as herring or mackerel. You could of course cook the dish in an ordinary large saucepan.

Recipe given to me by Senyor Juan Bonet Ribas of Cala Saladas

LLAGOSTA A LA CATALANA

Langouste à la catalane

1 large crawfish or 2 smaller ones,
4 onions, 12 grilled almonds,
1 carquinyoli *(a dry Catalan biscuit which you buy*
at Espluga on the way to the monastery of Poblet),
1 cube of chocolate,
1 small glass of vi ranci, *(very old wine which you will not find in England,*
but for which you can substitute sherry), olive oil.

Cover the bottom of a large pan with a quarter of an inch of oil. Grate the onions, put them into the pan, brown them lightly.

Cut up your live *langouste* into, say, three-inch slices, put them into the pan, salt them and stir carefully.

Then add the *picada* which is made thus:

Pound in a mortar the chocolate, the grilled almonds and the *carquinyoli*. Dilute with the *vi ranci* or sherry. If the langouste has any eggs pound these with the other ingredients. Cook for half an hour. Stir very lightly, otherwise there is a danger of the flesh coming away from the shell.

MUSCLOS
Mussels

For four people: 4 lbs of mussels,
2 onions, 3 ripe tomatoes,
$1/2$ a coffee-spoonful of paprika,
a clove of garlic, parsley, salt, pepper, oil.

Wash the mussels thoroughly, open them by putting them in a large covered pan on a hot flame. Throw away the empty shells and dispose those which contain the mussels in a large flat dish. Prepare a *sofregit* by heating three soup-spoonfuls of olive oil in a pan: hash the onions very fine and brown them in the oil, then add the tomatoes, peeled and crushed and cook for half an hour on a low flame so that the liquor from the tomatoes evaporates. Add the paprika, garlic chopped fine and the chopped parsley. Pour this sauce over the mussels. The dish can be eaten hot or cold.

RAP A LA MARINERA

Baudroie à la marinière

A large angler-fish,
$1/2$ a coffee-spoonful of powdered pimento,
a handful of pine-kernels,
a clove of garlic, parsley, olive oil.

Cut up the body of the fish into slices about an inch thick. Fry lightly on each side in oil. Remove the fish from the pan and stir the flour into the remaining oil as for a roux. When it begins to brown add the pimento, always stirring with a wooden spoon. Put the fish slices back in the pan and barely cover with cold water. Pound the pine-kernels in a mortar and when finely ground, grind the garlic and the chopped parsley. Put this *picada* into the pan, cover with a lid and cook for five minutes after it comes to the boil.

Rap: in English angler-fish, frog-fish, toad-fish, sea-devil, an ugly fish with a big head, native of the Mediterranean. See *sopa de rap* for what to do with the head. I am sure you could substitute any fish with firm flesh and large head, for these two recipes.

ROMESCO I

A piquant sauce for grey mullet, bream, sea bass, John Dory, cod, monkfish, etc.

For any of these fishes: a good slice of bread, 3 cloves of garlic,
3 or 4 tomatoes grilled on a woodfire,
12 grilled almonds, a large glass of wine,
a soup-spoon of paprika, a very little hot chilli pepper,
a teaspoon of wine vinegar.

Put a little oil in a pan and fry the slice of bread. Pound this bread in a large mortar or basin and add all the remaining ingredients in the order indicated above, reducing the whole to a smooth paste.

Put this preparation in the oil where the bread has fried, for one minute only, stirring hard with a wooden spoon. Then place the mixture on the fish (already cut into substantial slices) and cook for about twenty minutes on a slow fire in a shallow pan. Almost every fishing village has a variant on this sauce.

ROMESCO II

A sauce for fish grilled on a woodfire or on top of the range

40 grilled almonds, 3 cloves of garlic grilled on wood embers,
a small slice of raw onion,
1 carquinyoli (a dry Catalan biscuit),
1 teaspoon of sweet paprika, chopped parsley,
a very slight quantity of hot red chilli pepper,
3 or 4 large tomatoes grilled on a wood fire,
a teaspoon of wine vinegar, olive oil.

Put all these ingredients in a large mortar in the order indicated, pounding vigorously so that everything is reduced to a molecular state. Bind with oil and stir with a wooden spoon.

SARDINES EN ESCABETX
Marinated sardines

For 1 lb of fresh sardines use a whole head of garlic,
a few bay leaves, a large glass of wine vinegar,
a small teaspoonful of sweet powdered pimento, oil.

Clean the sardines and fry them in a little olive oil.

Put them in an earthenware dish and cover with the following marinade:

Brown the garlic unpeeled in a separate pan in olive oil, adding the bay leaves. As soon as the garlic cloves are well browned add the sweet pimento, stir for a minute or so, then pour in the vinegar and bring to the boil.

Pour this concoction over the sardines and leave the dish covered in a cool place. As this dish will keep for more than a week —in fact, the longer it marinates the better— it is worth doubling the quantities given here.

SARSUELA
Various fish and shellfish cooked in a highly spiced sauce

For the sofregit: *one onion, three tomatoes, oil.*
For the picada: *a handful of almonds, 2 sprigs of parsley,*
2 garlic cloves, ground black pepper.

Fish per head: *a slice of monkfish,*
a slice of whiting,
2 large prawns,
2 Dublin Bay prawns (in Catalan llagosti),
a small cuttlefish cut into slices,
6 or 7 mussels (washed, scrubbed, bearded).

Make a *sofregit* with finely chopped onion browned first in oil, adding the peeled tomatoes and cooking for half an hour to reduce. When ready add the *picada* made by pounding the almonds, the garlic, the chopped parsley and a generous quantity of ground black pepper. This mixture should cook in a wide flat pan (or *paella*). Put in all the fish with a very little water and cook for ten minutes covering the pan. A minute or two before serving add a few drops of *pernod*.

PAELLA

1/2 a chicken cut into small pieces,
the upper portion of some cutlets of pork, about 1/2 a lb,
2 medium-sized cuttlefish,
1 lb of mussels, (scrubbed and bearded),
a small crayfish per person,
1 coffee-cup of rice for each person and 3 times the volume of water,
6 or 7 soup-spoons of oil,
2 or 3 onions, finely chopped, 1 lb of peeled tomatoes,
1/4 lb of peas or French beans.

Put the oil into the *paella* and brown the chicken well, remove the pieces and put them in a dish. Now brown the pork cut into small pieces in the same oil. Remove the pork and brown the cuttlefish. Likewise the crayfish.

Heat the water, salt it in a separate pot with the peas or beans. Meanwhile brown the finely hashed onions in the *paella,* add the peeled tomatoes, crush them in the pan and cook gently for half an hour.

When this *sofregit is* ready put in two more tablespoons of olive oil, and the un-washed rice, fry it for five minutes and keep stirring so that the rice absorbs the oil. (You should turn up the gas and cook the rice more quickly.) After five minutes add the boiling water with the peas or beans. From this time on do not stir the rice. Put in the pan all the previously fried ingredients at the same time as the boiling water, as well as the mussels. Cook for twenty minutes and serve.

This is the classical Catalan *paella* which, I think, can easily be made in England. The great difficulty is to find a suitable cuttlefish. You can if you like add a pimento. In fact, in my opinion, you can add anything you like to the *paella* but never olives.

MEAT, POULTRY AND GAME

CAP-I-POTA
Calf's head and knuckle of beef

CARN ESTOFADA AMB PRUNES I PATATES
Stewed steak with prunes and potatoes

CONILL AMB PRUNES I PINYONS
Rabbit with prunes and pine-kernels

CONILL AMB CARGOLS I SALSA XOCOLATA
Rabbit with snails and chocolate sauce

ESCUDELLA: CARN D'OLLA
The Catalan *pot-au-feu*

LLOMILLO ARREBOSSAT
Fillet of pork fried in bread-crumbs

PERDIU AMB COL
Partridge with cabbage

PERDIU AMB VINAGRE
Partridge with vinegar

POLLASTRE AMB SAMFAINA
Chicken *en ratatouille*

POLLASTRE FARCIT
Stuffed roast chicken

TRIPES A LA CATALANA
Tripe *à la catalane*

CAP-I-POTA
Calf's head and knuckle of beef

1 lb of calf's head, 1 lb of knuckle of beef,
1 onion, 2 tomatoes, a large spoonful of red paprika pepper,
1 glass of white wine,
4 almonds, 2 cloves of garlic,
1 lb of potatoes.

Thoroughly wash the calf's head.

Simmer the veal and beef in salted water for one and a half hours, strain the broth, and cut the meat into small pieces. In a *cocotte* brown the onion, add the peeled tomatoes, the red pepper and the white wine. Reduce well. Put in the pieces of meat and the potatoes cut into pieces, stir and add just enough broth to cover. Cook for half an hour, occasionally stirring. Cook with the lid on. Just before serving pound the almonds with the garlic and put this in the pot, perhaps rinsing the mortar with a little of the sauce.

CARN ESTOFADA AMB PRUNES I PATATES
Stewed steak with prunes and potatoes

2 lbs of lean stewing steak, 1 onion,
3 cloves of garlic, 2 tomatoes,
a liqueur-glass of Spanish brandy,
1/2 teaspoon of sweet paprika pepper, a very little cinnamon,
1 large spoonful of flour, a bouquet garni,
1 1/2 large glasses of water, a large glass of white wine,
1/2 lb of prunes, 2 small potatoes per head, oil.

Cut the beef into substantial pieces, heat some oil in a pan, brown the pieces quickly on a hot flame, remove them and put in a pot. Cut the onion into several pieces and brown in the same oil with the garlic cloves, unpeeled. Then add the tomatoes peeled and crushed, the wine and the brandy. Reduce considerably over a slow fire, and add the sweet paprika pepper, the cinnamon, the flour very sparingly, (or a bar of grated chocolate) and the *bouquet garni.* Mix these ingredients with the sauce and pour in the water.

When this sauce is properly combined pour it over the meat in the pot. Cook slowly for two hours.

Simmer the prunes, which should be soaked in water in advance, for half an hour before the meal is served. Cut the potatoes into small cubes and fry in oil. Add these and the well-drained prunes to the dish in which you serve this stew.

The French and the Italians and perhaps the Spaniards laugh at us for serving mint sauce with mutton but in Catalan cooking it is almost impossible to escape from this sour-sweet combination.

CONILL AMB PRUNES I PINYONS
Rabbit with prunes and pine-kernels

A rabbit cut into pieces, 1 onion, 2 large tomatoes ripe and peeled,
thyme, bay leaf, a glass of wine,
12 skinned almonds, a clove of garlic, a few peppercorns,
1 lb of prunes and $^1/_2$ lb of pine-kernels,
salt and oil.

Fry the rabbit in six tablespoonfuls of oil and brown well. Remove from the pan onto a plate. Cut the onion finely, brown in the oil, add the tomatoes, crush them and cook for half an hour. Replace the rabbit in the pan, add the thyme, bay leaf and cook gently for two hours.

After an hour add the glass of wine.

In the meantime pound in a mortar the almonds, the clove of garlic and a few peppercorns. Add this *picada* to the dish a quarter of an hour before it is ready. The prunes which should be soaked the night before are put in a separate saucepan in cold water and cooked for half an hour. After a quarter of an hour put the pine-kernels into the same pan. Drain the prunes and pine-kernels and add to the dish of rabbit a few minutes before serving. The prunes are never stoned.

I think most of these ingredients can be procured in England but an 'English' rabbit which is usually a horrible refrigerated Australian beast is no good. Either breed rabbits yourself or try to shoot one of the few which have escaped the plague.

Recipe given to me by Senyora Solé, Restaurant Pi, Vendrell

CONILL AMB CARGOLS I SALSA XOCOLATA
Rabbit with snails and chocolate sauce

A rabbit, 2 lbs of snails, a veal-bone, a few necks and feet of chickens,
3 onions, 2 carrots, olive oil,
10 cloves of garlic, 2 dry biscuits, 5 or 6 almonds, 8 hazel-nuts,
some hot fresh capsicums (in Catalan called bitxo)*, five or six very ripe tomatoes,*
a small glass of brandy, a bar of bitter chocolate, black pepper,
a little nutmeg grated, a segment of red chilli pepper, salt.

Prepare a broth with one and a half pints of water, the veal-bone, the necks and feet of chickens, an onion and the carrots. Simmer this broth for two hours. Cut the rabbit into a number of pieces and brown it in oil in a *sautoir* for about a quarter of an hour, turning often. Remove the pieces from the pan.

Preparation of the snails: Put them in a bowl, sprinkle with a handful of rock-salt and a little vinegar. Stir vigorously for some minutes. Rinse them in water, changing the water several times until it is clear. Then put them in a vessel with water to cover, thyme, bay leaves and other herbs. Place the pot on the fire and simmer for five minutes. Put on one side. Pound finely in a mortar the ten cloves of garlic and fry in the same pan as the rabbit has browned, having first re-heated the oil. Have ready the *picada* which is prepared in the following manner: pound finely in the mortar first the almonds, then the hazel-nuts and then the biscuits. Throw this mixture into the pan with two small onions finely cut. Continue to stir making sure there is sufficient oil. Then add the tomatoes peeled and crushed and a small glass of brandy. Let it bubble for a few minutes. Now add the chocolate finely scraped. Stir vigorously so that the sauce thickens almost as if for a mayonnaise. In this sauce put the snails and the pieces of rabbit. Add the hot capsicums finely cut and a pinch of nutmeg and pepper, this of course at the same time as you put in the snails and the rabbit. Just cover with the broth, stir from time to time and simmer without a lid for about forty minutes. See that it is sufficiently salted.

Serve very hot. You can if you wish put in some finely cut potatoes. This is a dish from the district of Ampurda and if you have had the patience to prepare it you will lick your fingers, in the literal sense of the phrase for the only way to eat the snails is to hold the snail-shells in your hand and extract the snails with a toothpick.

Recipe given to me by Senyor Freixes

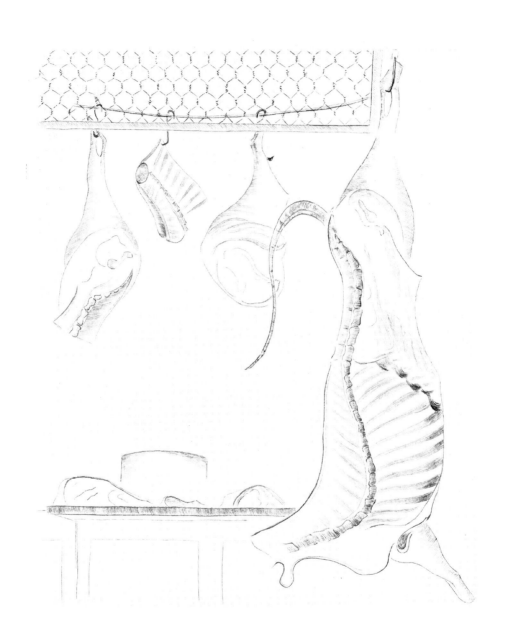

ESCUDELLA: CARN D'OLLA
The Catalan *pot-au-feu*

¹/₂ a chicken, 1 lb of stewing veal,
a white and a dark botifarra *(Catalan blood sausage),*
a small ham bone,
2 onions, 4 carrots, a little celery, 2 leeks,
a small green cabbage, ¹/₂ lb of chick-peas,
roughly 2 potatoes per person.

For the pilota *(dumplings): 2 cloves of garlic, parsley, 1 egg,*
a handful of bread-crumbs, ¹/₂ lb of sausage meat.
For the soup: ¹/₂ lb of small round macaroni.

The chick-peas need soaking in water with a pinch of bicarbonate overnight. Rinse them and give them a preliminary cooking for two hours. Put them in a deep tall sauce-pan *(marmite),* half fill it with water, bring to the boil and then put in the chicken, the veal, the ham bone, the onions, carrots, celery and leeks. Cook gently for an hour and a half, then add the cabbage and potatoes and the *botifarra* and cook for a further twenty minutes.

Meanwhile prepare the *pilota* by combining in a bowl the garlic, finely chopped, the sausage meat, the bread-crumbs and chopped parsley, and the whole raw egg. Mix well and form into the shape of two small rolls of bread. Flour them and cook for fifteen minutes in the communal pot.

Strain the soup from the pot into another pan and cook the macaroni in it for fourteen minutes, while keeping the meat and vegetables warm. Serve the soup first, then the meat and vegetables.

This is a very elaborate *pot-au-feu. Botifarra is* the name for several kinds of Catalan sausages. I suppose the dark sausage is something like a French *boudin noir* (blood sausage) which can be bought in Soho. Practically everything else can be found in England. This would be a good Sunday dinner for eight people, and as a small Catalan family usually consists of at least eight persons it will not be too much.

LLOMILLO ARREBOSSAT
Fillet of pork fried in bread-crumbs

1 fillet of pork,
one egg, bread-crumbs, salt, pepper.

Cut the fillet of pork into quarter of an inch slices. Beat up the egg with salt and pepper and dip the fillets of pork first in the egg and then in the bread-crumbs. Fry in very hot oil. Drain.

According to the season this is served either with cooked haricot beans or aubergines, or with a kind of mushroom, *Lactarius deliciosus,* which you certainly won't find in England unless you have a friend who is a mycologist. In Catalan these mushrooms are called *rovellóns.*

PERDIU AMB COLS
Partridge with cabbage

2 partridges, lard, 3 cloves of garlic, half an onion, 2 ripe tomatoes,
a handful of pine-kernels, parsley, salt,
a large green cabbage, 1 egg, 2 soup-spoons of flour, 1 glass of water, oil.

Coat the partridges with lard and roast them whole in a very gentle oven for an hour and a half. When they are cooked cut them into two or four pieces according to their size.

To prepare their sauce: Add a little more lard, say a soup-spoonful to the dish in which the partridges have roasted. Put the cloves of garlic cut fine into the pan, the half onion finely cut, and when they have browned add the two peeled tomatoes. This should be done on top of the stove. Meanwhile pound the pine-kernels in a mortar with the chopped parsley and stir this *picada* into the *sofregit*. When this sauce has simmered for about half an hour put the partridges in the pan with a lid on and finish cooking in the oven for half an hour, very slow oven. Separate the leaves of the cabbage and boil for ten minutes. Drain and quench with cold water, drain again. Take each leaf separately, fold and roll up each one into the shape of a small sausage. Beat an egg up in a plate with two soup-spoonfuls of flour and a glass of water. Dip the cabbage in this mixture and fry in oil. When well fried put them into the pan in which the partridges are cooking, for a quarter of an hour before serving.

NOTE: After having made the *sofregit* etc., the dish should be cooked very slowly with the lid on. Personally, I should use a *cocotte en fonte* indispensable for all slow cooking and obtainable I believe from Elizabeth David in Chelsea. In Catalonia this dish is prepared in an earthenware pot, but then the tempo of cooking like that of life is slower than with us.

These two partridge recipes were given to me
by Senyora Solé, Restaurant Pi, Vendrell

PERDIU AMB VINAGRE
Partridge with vinegar

This is made exactly like *perdiu amb cols* (see previous page) but the cabbage is replaced by one and a half pounds of little onions which are blanched, browned in oil and cooked in a separate dish for half an hour in the oven, and three soup-spoonfuls of wine vinegar which are added to the dish a quarter of an hour before serving. The onions can be served separately or, at the last moment put into the *cocotte* as a garnish for the partridges.

POLLASTRE FARCIT
Stuffed roast chicken

A tender chicken, and for the stuffing, $^1/_2$ lb of apples,
the same quantity of prunes, 4 ounces of pine-kernels,
salt, a soup-spoon of lard,
and oil in the dish and on the chicken.

Soak the prunes for one or two hours. Stuff the bird with the apples peeled and cored, the prunes unstoned, the pine-kernels left whole and the lard. Rub the bird with salt and anoint it with oil. Cook for one hour and a half in a hot oven. Turn and baste often. The apples can be replaced by the same amount of sausage meat.

POLLASTRE AMB SAMFAINA
Braised chicken *en ratatouille*

A tender chicken, 4 or 5 onions, 1 lb of tomatoes,
2 green peppers, one aubergine per head, oil.

Put in a cast-iron pan some finely chopped onions with sufficient oil and when browned add two peeled tomatoes. Cut up the chicken into four sections and put them into the casserole when the *sofregit* has reduced. This process as usual takes about half an hour. Cook the chicken for about an hour in this sauce, basting and turning occasionally.

In a frying pan separately fry two or three onions finely chopped in olive oil, and before they are too brown put in the peppers which you have cored, seeded and sliced. Cook slowly until tender.

Then put in the remainder of the tomatoes. Season.

In another pan fry the aubergines cut into slices, and when cooked drain them and put in the same pan as the onions and peppers. Remove the chicken from the casserole for a moment. Put the vegetable contents of the frying pan into the casserole in which the chicken has cooked and replace the pieces of chicken. Simmer very slowly for half an hour with the lid on.

TRIPES A LA CATALANA
Tripe *à la catalane*

2 lbs of uncooked tripe, 2 lbs of potatoes, 3 onions, 5 tomatoes, oil,
a good pinch of red chilli pepper, 3 ounces of grated Gruyere cheese.

To clean the tripe soak in vinegar and water for some time and rinse. When thoroughly cleaned put in a pan with cold water, add salt and boil for one hour. Drain and cut into pieces one to one and a half inches thick.

While the tripe is cooking cut the potatoes into dice and fry them in olive oil until they are golden. Drain. Cut the three onions in large slices, fry until brown. Peel and crush the five tomatoes and put them in a pan with the red chilli pepper and plenty of oil until the juice has evaporated.

Then add the onions to this sauce. Take a dish which goes into the oven and put the tripe and potatoes at the bottom, cover it with the tomato and onion sauce, sprinkle with grated Gruyere and cook for fifteen minutes.

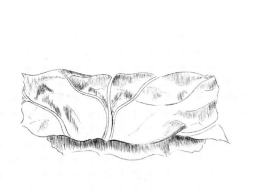

SALAD AND VEGETABLES

AMANIDA
Salad

ALBERGÍNIES
Aubergines

CIGRONS GUISATS
Chick-peas

ESCALIVADA
This is a braise in the original meaning of that word,
i. e. cooking on glowing embers

ESPINACS AMB PANSES I PINYONS
Spinach with raisins and pine-kernels

FAVES A LA CATALANA
Broad beans *à la catalane*

MONGETES BLANQUES
Haricot beans

PATATES I MONGETES
Potatoes and beans

PATATES VÍDUES
'Widowed' potatoes

ROVELLÓNS
Lactarius deliciosus

AMANIDA
Salad

2 large sweet Spanish onions,
1 large tomato per person,
preferably not overripe, some olives,
1 or 2 green peppers,
a cos lettuce and some radishes.

Cut the lettuce to form a bed at the bottom of the salad bowl, cut the tomatoes into three transverse sections and lay them on the lettuce, then the onions sliced into fine rings; remove the seeds from the peppers and cut them into strips, scatter the olives in the bowl and the radishes, which, by making two vertical incisions in each one and a third vertical cut at right angles to these can be made to open like a flower.

Each guest helps himself to salad and seasons it on his own plate with coarse salt, oil and vinegar, but no Catalan ever puts vinegar on tomatoes.

ALBERGÍNIES
Aubergines

Cut the aubergines into small slices without peeling, salt the slices and leave them for an hour to remove the excess of water. Rinse them in cold water to remove some of the salt, dry them in a cloth and throw into hot oil for about five minutes. Serve immediately.

CIGRONS GUISATS
Chick-peas

1 lb of chick-peas,
olive oil, 1 onion, 1 tomato,
a little flour, parsley, black pepper, some of the liquor
in which the chick-peas have cooked.
For the picada: *8 pounded almonds, a few pine-kernels,*
chopped parsley and garlic all ground fine in a mortar.

Soak the chick-peas overnight with a pinch of bicarbonate. Rinse them and boil till tender, adding a little salt, for about four hours. Heat the oil in the pan, put in one onion finely hashed, a clove of garlic and parsley chopped. When these begin to brown put in a ripe peeled tomato. When this has simmered for a while add a coffee-spoonful of flour and stir until it thickens, moistening with a few spoonfuls of liquor in which the chick-peas have cooked. Then throw in the chick-peas, well drained, the black pepper and add the *picada*.

Chick-peas prepared in this way are sometimes served with slices of hard-boiled eggs.

ESCALIVADA

A braise in the original meaning of
that word, i.e. cooking on glowing embers

3 aubergines, 2 large green peppers,
4 very ripe tomatoes, 4 Spanish onions.

Make a woodfire and when it dies down place the vegetables directly on the embers. The onions cook much more slowly than the other vegetables, about one hour. Turn them from time to time until the skin is well burnt. When you judge that they are cooked, remove them from the fire and take away the charred skins. Cut up the peppers and aubergines lengthways, likewise the onions, put them on a dish, salt them and anoint with plenty of olive oil and a little chopped garlic. The tomatoes should be served separately. *Escalivada* is served as an *entrée*.

ESPINACS AMB PANSES I PINYONS
Spinach with raisins and pine-kernels

4 lbs of spinach, a large handful of raisins
and a handful of pine-kernels, oil and salt.

Wash the spinach, put it in a casserole with no water and a little salt, set it on a moderate heat for ten minutes, turning it about two or three times. When the spinach has rendered its liquor drain it.

Put four soup-spoons of oil in a pan and when it is hot throw in the raisins and let them swell. This takes about two minutes, stirring the while. Put in the pine-kernels which brown in a moment, and throw in the spinach. Heat for five to six minutes.

The whole operation after having initially prepared the spinach should take only a few minutes and is best done just before sitting down to a meal. If spinach is not available, the same dish can be made with spinach beet which must be cleaned and any stringy portions removed. Another Catalan dish doubtless dating from the Middle Ages when sweet ingredients were so much used in cooking.

FAVES A LA CATALANA
Broad beans *à la catalane*

4 lbs of young broad beans, shelled, 1 onion, 1 tomato,
2 spoonfuls of oil, 2 spoonfuls of lard,
1 slice of fat bacon cut into dice,
the same quantity of botifarra negra *(Catalan black sausage)*
cut into rounds, 1 coffee-spoonful of red paprika pepper,
a little black pepper, a square of bitter chocolate,
a branch of mint or, if not, a very small glass of unsweetened anis.

In a lidded *marmite* put the oil, chop the onion fine and slightly brown it. Add the peeled tomato, the lard, the bacon, the rounds of sausage, the red pepper, the chocolate (grated) and the mint. Put in the beans, just cover with water and put on the lid. Cook very gently for three quarters of an hour to one hour depending on how tender are your broad beans. Look at this from time to time in case it dries up, in which case add a little water.

Of course you will find it difficult to get the Catalan sausage in London, and if you substitute *anis* for mint, you will find this simple Catalan dish an expensive one. Perhaps blood sausage *(boudin noir)* procurable in Soho could be a substitute for the *botifarra negra*.

MONGETES BLANQUES
Haricot beans

Soak overnight and cook the beans until tender. Drain well and put them into a pan of hot oil for five to ten minutes.

They should be a little browned.

PATATES I MONGETES
Potatoes and beans

2 medium-sized potatoes per person, a handful of French beans,
1 onion, salt, oil.

Cut the potatoes into four, put them in a saucepan of cold water, bring to the boil, salt. Ten minutes after the water boils put in the onion cut into two and the beans, topped and tailed. Let them boil for a quarter of an hour. Drain and serve. Each person helps himself to the quantity of oil that he thinks fit from the *setrill,* a special little bottle with a very fine spout.

This is a Catalan supper eaten every night by the peasants and it will not give you a nightmare. It is also called by them *verdura.* Cabbage can be substituted for French beans when these are out of season

PATATES VIDUES
'Widowed' potatoes

2 lbs of potatoes, 1 onion, 1 tomato,
1/4 coffee-spoonful of sweet pimento, a bay leaf.
For the picada: 4 grilled almonds,
a soup-spoonful of pine-kernels, a clove of garlic, oil.

Peel the potatoes and cut into thin slices. Chop up the onion fine, brown in oil in a *sautoir* and then add the peeled tomatoes. Crush the tomatoes, cook for five minutes, then put in the bay leaf and sweet pimento. Put in the sliced potatoes, cover with cold water and cook gently. When the potatoes are half cooked, say in a quarter of an hour, add the *picada* prepared in the following manner:

Pound the almonds and the pine-kernels and when these are pulverized put in the clove of garlic and continue to pound. Put this preparation in the pot in which the potatoes are cooking. Cover and cook for another quarter of an hour.

Recipe given to me by Anita Simal Llonch

ROVELLÓNS
Lactarius deliciosus

This mushroom is also to be found in England, growing often on the margins of coniferous woods in sandy soil. The Catalan name derives from *rovell* meaning rust, referring to its orange colour; the cap has concentric circles of a darker shade and is often stained with a greenish hue. When broken it exudes an orange milky juice.

Keep the mushrooms whole. Remove any debris that is attached to them, salt and oil them, then place them on a grill over a woodfire.

When they are cooked, five to ten minutes, serve with parsley and garlic finely chopped, and as much oil at the table as each person wants.

REFRIGERIS
Something to eat at any time of day

CALÇOTS
Onion shoots

PA AMB TOMÀQUET
Bread and tomatoes

CALÇOTS
Onion shoots

The word *calçots* comes from *calçar (chausser)*, to put on one's shoes, boots, stockings. During the time that the onion shoots are growing one dresses these shoots with earth in order to blanch them (like celery).

Cultivation of *calçots*:
Take some small Spanish onions and plant them with their bases just below the level of the soil in January. Allow them to grow to a respectable size which will take in Spain roughly until June. Remove them from the earth and keep them in a dry place until September which is their period of germination. In September plant them in a trench as for celery. Each onion should give seven or eight sprouts. As these sprouts appear earth them up. When they have reached the size of a very large leek (three to four inches across) cut them at the base of the shoot and trim the tops to make them all of equal size.

To cook them make a very large woodfire and put a grill on it as large as a spring mattress —I say this because some thirty persons eat thirty or forty onion shoots between them. Turn them over and thoroughly burn them on each side. To eat them, extract the shoots from the burnt exterior with your fingers. They are eaten with the following sauce and these are the ingredients for each person:

Two ounces of grilled almonds, two cloves of garlic (the head of garlic grilled on the woodfire), one clove of garlic not grilled, a pinch of red pepper, a little parsley, a little mint, salt, one grilled tomato skinned, vinegar if you like it and oil.

Pound all this in a mortar or a large pot beginning with the almonds and finally bind it with oil. The sauce should never be thick. Now dip the onion shoots in this sauce.

This is a pre-spring dish eaten only in the neighbourhood of Valls, in the open air under the almond trees in bloom. If it snows so much the better. This is only part of the feast, followed by roast chickens, mutton cutlets, every kind of sausage and of course plenty of wine drunk from the *porró*.

PA AMB TOMÀQUET
Bread with tomatoes

For each person cut a thick slice of country bread, cut a ripe tomato in two and crush it on both sides of the slice of bread. Salt the bread and thoroughly saturate with olive oil.

This is a typical Catalan preparation which can be eaten at any time of day. It is often accompanied with a slice of *jambon cru* or grilled salt herring (see *Arengada*).

As a variant you can lightly toast the bread and rub it with a clove of garlic saturating it with oil as above.

SWEETS

LA COCA DE LLARDONS
La tourte aux lardons

CREMA CREMADA
Crème brûlée

PANELLETS
Almond cakes

SALSA
Eivissenques Christmas Pudding

LA COCA DE LLARDONS
La tourte aux lardons

1 lb of fat cut from a jambon cru,
*cut into little dice and gently fried
for a few minutes in a pan to reduce some of the fat,
3 eggs, a cup of sugar, a pinch of cinnamon,
the grated rind of a lemon, a glass of sherry,
1 lb of flour, baker's yeast,
a glass of milk boiled with a stick
of vanilla, a few drops of anis,
1/4 lb of pine-kernels, a soup-spoonful of oil.*

Beat the eggs, amalgamate the sugar beating to a cream, put in the cinnamon and the grated lemon rind. Incorporate the *lardons* and then the sherry.

Sift a pound of plain flour into this mixture. Dissolve the yeast in a little of the milk and stir it in lightly, pour in the rest of the milk and add the *anis.* Add the pine-kernels. Put a very little oil in a round oven pan and spread the mixture in it, cook in a moderate oven for three quarters of an hour.

Coca is a generic word for flan, which may be sweet or savoury.

It can also be made with spinach and white beans and white sausage. In fact the possibilities of varying it are as many as the *pizza napolitana.*

CREMA CREMADA
Crème brûlée

4 egg yolks, 2 full tablespoons of flour, 1 pint of milk,
4 large tablespoonfuls of sugar, the rind of a lemon,
half a stick of cinnamon.

Beat up the yolks of the eggs with the sugar. Separately mix the flour with a little of the milk. Meanwhile infuse the cinnamon stick and lemon rind in the rest of the milk which having been heated should be allowed to cool. Strain it into the flour and milk paste, stirring the while, then gradually add this concoction to the egg yolks and sugar and bring to the boil, stirring vigorously all the time. Turn out the thickened custard into a flat dish. Next day sprinkle the custard copiously with powdered sugar.

Heat a salamander (or poker) until it is red hot and gently burn the sugar.

The custard itself must be made the day before.

PANELLETS
Almond cakes

2 lbs of shelled almonds, 1 lb 9 ozs of sugar,
1 packet of vanilla sugar,
2 or 3 potatoes, if they are small.

Soak the almonds in hot water for a few minutes and peel them. Spread them on a cloth and let them dry if possible for two days in the sun, then reduce them to a powder, a little at a time, in a large mortar. In Catalonia special grinding mills exist for this purpose.

Boil the potatoes in their skins and peel and mash well. Mix with the pounded almonds, adding the sugar and vanilla sugar.

Here I should explain that you can flavour this mixture in two ways, dividing it of course into two parts.

To one part you add a quarter of a pound of grated coconut, sold in Catalonia at pastry shops, and a small glass of *anis*. In the other half put a small glass of brandy with some orange or lemon essence. Form into little cakes and stick one or two almonds on top, or cover with pine-kernels. Heat the oven thoroughly and place the little cakes on a flat oiled tin. As soon as they are very lightly browned, after a few minutes, remove them and put in others.

SALSA
Eivissenques Christmas Pudding

1 1/2 lbs of almonds, skinned (by soaking for a few minutes in hot water)
and reduced to a fine powder in a mortar,
3 pints of hot water, 4 eggs, 2 sticks of cinnamon
(or 2 large spoonfuls of powdered cinnamon),
10 large spoonfuls of white sugar, a spoonful of salt,
4 spoonfuls of olive oil, a small spoonful of powdered saffron,
2 or 3 dry biscuits pounded.

Heat the water. Put the pounded almonds in the centre of a bowl, break four eggs into it and mix with the almond flour. Add sugar. Put this mixture in the saucepan and with a wooden spoon mix well with the hot water. Bring to the boil. Add the salt, the cinnamon and the pounded biscuits. After this mixture has cooked for an hour add the powdered saffron and the oil and cook for at least two hours.

This is the *Eivissenques* Christmas Pudding eaten only at Christmas. Like an English Christmas Pudding it can be prepared in advance. This is a very ancient dish probably brought to *Eivissa* (the Catalan name of the island of Ibiza) by the Phoenicians. I feel that the sugar has replaced what was originally honey. Pounding the almonds is not an easy operation in the absence of a special mill for the purpose. Otherwise use a pestle and mortar adding the almonds a little at a time. An old lady of *Eivissa* to whom I showed this recipe told me it is better to put chicken stock than water! This pudding is served by ladling out into separate bowls.

Recipe given to me by Senyor Juan Bonet Ribas of Cala Saladas

WINE

Of course wine is a necessary accompaniment to any Catalonian meal. You cannot imagine eating any of these dishes served with water, milk-coffee, a 'nice cup of tea' or even with coca-cola, the habit of which I regret to say is spreading in Catalonia.

Catalonia is, I believe, the second largest wine producing province in Spain. Those who are interested in the history of wine-making past and present should visit the Museum of Wine at Villafranca, almost unique in the world.

Catalonia roughly speaking begins at Perpignan and ends at Valencia so it can easily be imagined that the variety of wines is very large.

A SUMMER
AND AN AUTUMN DRINK

ORXATA D'AMETLLES
A non-alcoholic summer drink

LA BARREJA
A refreshing autumn drink

ORXATA D'AMETLLES
A non-alcoholic summer drink

105 almonds, 2 lbs of sugar,
a stick of cinnamon, a lemon rind and a 1/2 pint of water

Peel the almonds, spread them out on a cloth to dry for at least two days in the sun. Then in a special grinding mill, found in most Catalan houses, reduce them to a fine powder. Put this in a fine linen cloth and dip it into the water in a basin taking it out and pressing it until finally there is nothing more left in the cloth. Then add the cinnamon, the scraped lemon rind, the sugar well mixed, and put it on the fire. As soon as it reaches boiling point, cool and bottle.

LA BARREJA
A refreshing autumn drink

In a pint of muscatel wine put two small glasses of dry *anis*. Drink it preferably from a *porró* while eating figs.

In winter when there are no figs, you can substitute chocolate, a warming drink before going into the fields to collect olives.

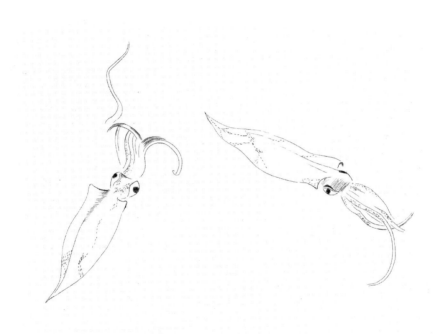

THE FEAST OF THE THREE FISHERMEN OF CALAFELL

There are three courses: First the potatoes and fish with the *allioli* sauce. This is called the fishermen's *romesco*.

Next the dish of rice called *arrossejat* is served.

And lastly for the third course the octopi, called in Catalan *pops.*

Four pounds of rock fishes (the names of most of these fishes are unknown in England, one is the *rascassa* familiar to visitors to the Mediterranean, the others are *corballs, rata, esparrall, sàlvia*), two pounds of very ripe tomatoes, two pounds of rice, eight pounds of potatoes, four heads of garlic, one pound of onions, four hot chilli peppers (dried), a slice of bread, two pounds of small octopi.

First of all take a plane to Barcelona, then drive to Calafell, then find your fishermen and go with them about four o'clock to Villanova and get them to choose the fish as it is landed.

When you return home get the fishermen to clean the rock fish and cut them into pieces, put them in a basin and salt well. Clean the octopi thoroughly and remove their ink. Peel and cut the potatoes into slices about an inch thick, cut the onions moderately fine. Peel the garlic and the tomatoes.

First course: The Fishermen's *romesco.* In a large upright saucepan *(marmite)* brown twelve cloves of garlic in oil; as soon as the garlic is brown put in two of the chilli peppers, opened but whole from which you have removed the seeds. After two or three minutes add the slice of bread. While the bread is browning remove the peppers and the cloves of garlic and pound very fine in a mortar. When the bread is browned put it in the mortar and reduce to a fine paste. Add to this mixture a very small glass of white wine. Continue stirring and fill the mortar with water. Now add the contents of the mortar to the *marmite* making sure that the oil is smoking hot. If the bread has absorbed too much oil, add some more. Add three more mortarfulls of water. Here I should say that in Catalonia a mortar is far larger than those usually found in England. Allow this mixture to boil hard. Now put in the potatoes, cook hard for ten minutes and then add the rock fish and six minutes later the *picada crua,* which is made in the following manner:

Pound two hot chilli peppers (seeded) in the mortar, add ten cloves of garlic and when finely pounded add a small glass of water. Put this mixture into the pan six minutes before the contents have finished cooking. Take the pot off the fire.

Prepare an *allioli* sauce to be served with the fish and potatoes. Pound twelve cloves of garlic very finely, add two drops of water, and stirring continually in one direction gradually add olive oil. When the oil begins to thicken add five drops of vinegar and continue to stir adding oil until the mortar is filled with this thick garlic mayonnaise. It seems incredible that one can make a mayonnaise without eggs but the Catalan fishermen can. Now pour the *allioli* into a sauce-boat and add to it about the same quantity of water which is first used to rinse out the mortar before incorporating it to thin the sauce.

Second course: *Arrossejat.* Take a wide but not too deep pan, put in some oil, slice up two large onions and cook them lightly, add the rice, not washed and let it cook very slowly stirring all the time until it has absorbed the oil and begins to turn a golden brown. Then add the liquor from the first pot in which the potatoes and rock fishes have cooked. This quantity of sauce should be sufficient to cook the rice but if you have any doubt add a little water, always remembering that one cup of rice requires three cups of liquid. Add a soup-spoonful of *allioli.* Cook for twenty minutes, stirring often. The rice should not be overcooked and must be quite dry.

Third course: White *pops.* In a pot boil a pint of water, throw the octopi into the pot and cook them for half an hour with the lid half off. Strain them. In another pot add oil and cook the remainder of the chopped onions allowing them to brown well, then add the peeled and crushed tomatoes; as usual reduce the sauce and in it cook the octopi for about half an hour.

Wash the meal down with *porró* after *porró* of local white wine and ask your fishermen to sing some of the songs of Catalonia. This is the last recipe in my book and is a meal to end all meals.

Note: *Corballs* in Latin is *Umbrina cirrhosa*, *rata* is *Uranoscopos scaber*, *esparrall* is *Sargus annularis*, and *sàlvia* is *Trachinus radiatus*.

ACKNOWLEDGMENTS
(1969)

The publication of this volume of Catalan recipes, which Irving Davis had compiled so eagerly, has been made possible by the enthusiastic cooperation of his friends, Patience Gray, Nicole Fenosa, Ariane Castaing and Lucien Scheler, with the warm encouragement and support of his step-daughter, Ianthe Carswell.

The author would have wished above all to thank Nicole Fenosa not only for the engravings which appear in this book but for her unfailing help, without which these recipes would never have been translated from the Catalan. He was also indebted to Senyora Anita Simal Llonch whose prowess as a cook was an inspiration in preparing this little book. Thanks are also due to Senyora Solé of Restaurant Pi, Vendrell, Senyor Juan Bonet Ribas of Cala Saladas, Senyor Freixes, for divulging some precious recipes.

GLOSSARY

ALBERGÍNIA	aubergine
ALLIOLI	garlic 'mayonnaise' made without egg yolks
AMANIDA	salad
AMB	with
AMETLLES	almonds
ARENGADA	dried salt herring
ARREBOSSAT	fried in bread-crumbs
ARROSSEJAT	fishermen's rice dish
BACALLÀ	salt cod
BARAT	mackerel
BARREJA	a mixed drink
BITXO	very hot capsicum
BOSC	woods
BOTIFARRA	Catalan sausage, the dark variety resembles a *boudin noir*
CALAMAR	squid
CALÇOTS	onion shoots
CALDERETA	earthenware pot or cauldron. (In Catalonia a dish often derives its name from the pot in which it is cooked.)
CAP	head
CARBASSA	pumpkin
CARGOLS	snails
CARN	meat
CARQUINYOLI	dry Catalan biscuit; sometimes used for thickening a sauce
CARXOFA	artichoke
CASACA	batter
CIGRONS	chick-peas
COCA	tourte, cake
COL	cabbage
CONILL	rabbit
CREMA	custard
CREMADA	burnt
CRUA	raw
DOLÇOS	sweet
ESCABETX	marinade
ESCALIVADA	braise; the generic name for anything braised in the embers of a woodfire
ESCUDELLA	the name for a cooking pot and the soup which is cooked in it
ESPÀRRECS	asparagus
ESPINACS	spinach
ESQUEIXAT	flaked
ESTOFADA	stew

FARCIT	stuffed
FARIGOLA	thyme
FAVES	broad beans
FERRAT	fried
FORN	oven
GUISATS	simmered
LLAGOSTA	*langouste*
LLARDON	lardoon
LLAUNA	a shallow tin dish
LLOMILLÓ	fillet
MACARRONS	macaroni
MARINERA	in the fishermen's way
MONGETES	beans
MUSCLOS	mussels
NEGRA	black
OLLA	earthenware *marmite* and the *pot-au-feu* cooked in it
ORXATA	a summer drink
OU	egg
PA	bread
PAELLA	a shallow two-handled pan which has given its name to the dish of fish, shellfish, rice and other things which is cooked in it
PANELLETS	almond cakes
PANSES	raisins
PATATES	potatoes
PEIX	fish
PERDIU	partridge
PICADA	*coup de bec;* the characteristic 'bite' given to many dishes by the addition of pounded garlic, almonds, pine-kernels, etc., towards the end of cooking
PICANTS	piquant
PILOTA	dumpling
PINYONS	pine-kernels
PLANXA	iron plank
POLLASTRE	chicken
POPS	small octopi
PORRÓ	glass vessel with tapered spout for wine drinking
POTA	foot
PRUNES	prunes
RANCI	very old
RAP	*baudroie,* angler fish, sea-devil
REFRIGERIS	something to eat at any time of day
ROMESCO	fishermen's sauce
ROVELLÓ	*lactarius deliciosus,* species of mushroom
SALSA	sauce
SAMFAINA	*ratatouille,* vegetables stewed in oil

SARSUELA	literally "Operette"
SETRILL	a little glass bottle with a fine spout for serving olive oil
SOBRESSADA	a smoked Catalan sausage
SOFREGIT	*fricassée,* under-fried from *sofregir*, to underfry
SOPA	soup
TOMAQUET	tomato
TRAMPA	trick
TRIPES	tripe
TRUITA	omelette
TUNA	tunny-fish
VERDURA	a dish of potatoes and French beans
VI	wine
VINAGRE	vinegar
XANGUET	whitebait
XOCOLATA	chocolate

IRVING DAVIS

Memories

Joseph Irving Davis

'L'air est plein du frisson des choses qui s'enfuient…'

Ch. Baudelaire

L'une des figures les plus représentatives et les plus originales de l'univers biblio-philique, notre cher Irving Davis, est mort le 1er mai dernier. Né à Londres le 6 février 1889, Davis avait fait ses études classiques au célèbre St Paul's [et] Sidney Sussex College de Cambridge.

Irrésistiblement attiré par l'Italie, dès l'obtention de ses titres universitaires et prise de sa décision de devenir libraire, il partit pour la Toscane et s'associait en 1911 avec Guiseppe Orioli. Deux librairies à leurs noms furent alors simultanément ouvertes, l'une à Londres, l'autre à Florence. Après une vingtaine d'années, devenu seul pro-priétaire de la firme, Davis, sans pour autant renoncer au charme de la vie italienne, concentra son activité commerciale à Londres où il publia 170 catalogues de livres anciens, voués essentiellement à la description des chefs-d'oeuvre littéraires de la Renaissance italienne ainsi qu'aux éditions originales des meilleurs textes anciens médicaux et scientifiques. Collectionneurs, bibliothécaires et libraires sont infiniment redevables à ces catalogues si riches en documentation et en renseignements biblio-graphiques. En 1955, sous le parrainage de la National Book League, Davis organisa à Londres une remarquable Exposition du Livre italien; à cette occasion, le gouverne-ment de Rome le décora et lui décerna le titre de Commendatore.

Davis, qui pour des raisons de santé n'avait pas été mobilisé dans le service armé, fut, pendant la première Guerre mondiale, employé au Ministère britannique de la guerre, dans le service du chiffre.

Il possédait une collection personelle de livres italiens à figures, parmi les plus rares. S'étant lié au cours de son existence florentine avec les intellectuels qui composaient avant 1914 la colonie anglaise de Toscane, il était devenue l'ami de Norman Douglas, de Reginald Turner, de Max Beerbohm. Davis, qui a consacré à Tammaro de Marinis, son illustre confrère de Florence, une étude amicale et charmante, laisse des *Mémoires* inédits. Gastronome et amateur des grands crûs, il a publié un ouvrage estimé sur les vins de France.

Durant 60 ans, il parcourut l'Europe, en quête de livres précieux, mais ne se rendit jamais aux USA. Libraire international par excellence, mais aussi esprit cosmopolite et plein de fantaisie, un Barnabooth qui eût été [quelque] peu bohême. Généreux par surcroît; c'est ainsi qu'au cours de la guerre civile d'Espagne, il avait pour les enfants de Barcelone assiégée, fait l'acquisition de médicaments qu'en camionnette il achemina lui-même à bon port.

Après notre libération, en 1945, il revint régulièrement à Paris, passant de fréquentes soirées, de Montparnasse à Montmartre, de la Boule Blanche à la Villa ou la Cabane Cubaine, dans ces cabarets que hantent des mulâtresses au rire enfantin. A l'heure de la fermeture, à peine las mais contraint de partir, il se retrouvait récitant du John Donne sur le seuil blanchissant, dans la fraîcheur de l'aube. Sa compagne d'un soir le regardant avec indulgence de ses yeux de gazelle africaine, tous deux s'échappaient alors dans un taxi crépusculaire.

Lucien Scheler
(Bulletin de la Librairie
ancienne et moderne,
n° 97, Juillet-Août, 1967)

Bouquiniste

I am now sixty-five. My present life is uninteresting and my future life – well, let me hope that if I live ten years more I shall be able to say these last ten years have been uninteresting and nothing worse.

So I turn to the past. The past, what is it? A vast rubbish heap.

Once a week, or if you are a tidy man, once a day, you put the debris in the dustbin. It disappears; it is dumped somewhere and we do not trouble to enquire where. The Assyrians, the Egyptians, the Greeks did this; the Romans made a huge hill of broken crockery, the Monte Testaccio. Earth has covered it, plants and grass have overgrown it, but there it is for archaeologists to dig into and perhaps find something very precious and worth preserving, but something that has suffered a change, an object which is not what it was. The statue is armless, the gilded bronze has lost its gold and acquired a different and perhaps more beautiful patina from its long burial underground.

All this is to explain that there will be very little objective truth in my reminiscences. I think all famous writers of autobiographies, Rousseau, Casanova, and even my own partner Pino Orioli, whose memoirs pleased so many of his contemporaries, were liars – or should I say creative artists?

But as Sir Thomas Browne wrote: "'What is truth?' said jesting Pilate, and did not pause for an answer" – so quite cheerfully I shall prod in the dustbin of my own past and see what comes to light.

Madame de Marcelli's *pension*. I don't suppose I have thought of this place for forty years. I must have stayed there when I was still an undergraduate at Cambridge, wishing to improve my French in order to qualify as a student interpreter, a branch of the Consular Service which I think no longer exists.

The *pension*, if I remember rightly, was in a turning on the right, off the *rue Faubourg Montmartre*, above the horseshoe-shaped *rue la Ferrière* where nearly every house was a brothel. It was on the second floor. What I remember of it most vividly is the smell of the concierge's life, that unforgettable odour of cabbage soup which, like the smell of Gauloises will always evoke Paris for me and the sickly underground complexion of those troglodytes.

Madame and her husband, the concierges established by Napoleon to report to the police on the comings and goings of the tenants, still persist, so does the smell of her cooking.

Madame de Marcelli, who pronounced her name in the French style, 'Marselli', was a florid blonde from Montauban. Her husband was an Italian with a noble Titianesque face and a long white beard, a silent man who had fought when young in the Papal army when Garibaldi besieged Rome, from which Historians may deduce his age.

I cannot remember if the food was good or bad. In those days I was less interested in the table than I am now, but I know that what I ate was to me surprising and abundant, with *vin à discrétion* and all for five francs a day. Besides myself there must have been five or six *pensionnaires*. The persistent obscenity of their conversation at table seemed to me very strange. Everything was the object of a phallic allusion, but most jokes were lost on me. I can remember one of the *pensionnaires*, a member of the Sûreté, and like most of the police force a Corsican, dark, small and with a face deeply pock-marked. We dined at 12 o'clock.

"Quelle heure avez-vous?"

"J'ai midi!"

At one o'clock we finished dinner. *"Quelle heure avez-vous, Monsieur?"*

"Ah, Madame, j'ai toujours midi!"

I was joined by my friend Phillip Woolf and a Pauline friend Morant who is caricatured in Orioli's book and I think by Orioli himself. One evening we went to the Bal Tabarin, where we drank a quantity of a sickly liqueur called *cordial Médoc* which my friend Flecker had introduced me to at Cambridge. As a result, Morant became quarrelsome and was with difficulty disentangled from a dispute with a Frenchman whom he had challenged to a duel the next morning in the Bois.

Most vividly I remember the end of the evening, a dance, or rather a procession round the dancing floor by a number of elderly Frenchmen *all* with beards and looking like gnomes in a Walt Disney picture, their hands on each other's shoulders.

After having rescued my quarrelsome friend I said we must finish the evening at the Rat Mort. In those days I was what would be now described as a 'highbrow' and had read George Moore's *Confessions of a Young Man* with great enjoyment. If anyone now alive has read the book they will remember that the Rat Mort was in the '80s the meeting place of artists and men of letters. Here George Moore claimed – I do not know with how much truth – that he hobnobbed with Manet, Degas *et hoc genus omne*. But by the early years of this century it had changed very considerably.

It was a melancholy little café on the Place Pigalle with, I think, a room upstairs where you could drink champagne and see a show. Seated at the tables on the ground floor were a few gloomy whores. Of course in our semi-drunken state we soon became their victims and there they were sitting at our table drinking *coupes de champagne* and *menthe à l'eau*.

My own partner was a tall flat-chested blonde with long horse-like teeth, the caricature of an Englishwoman as the French then imagined them. They hadn't much time to waste.

"Viens chez moi, mon chou, tu seras mieux."

"We must get out of this," I said.

"But how?"

"Follow me and I will show you."

We went into the Place Pigalle followed by our companions.

"When I say run, run," and run we did as fast as our young legs could carry us, followed by the curses which I could not understand, as far as la Trinité and there we painfully climbed the hill to Montmartre, to Madame de Marcelli's *pension*.

"Cordon s'il vous plait", and so to bed.

ITALY

'Italiam petinus' has always been my broth as it was that of Aeneas. I would have wished to exile myself to that country like Byron, Shelley, Browning, or like our latest English exiles, Douglas, Lawrence, Huxley, Beerbohm – in spite of currency restrictions these exiles persist, the English in Italy still, but I suppose I had not sufficient artistic talent and, as the Italians say, *mancavano i quattrini*, I had no money. "Open my heart, and you will see 'graved upon it, Italy."

The first time I came near to that country which I have loved so much was when I was twelve. My mother, father, sister and I went for a fortnight's holiday to Lucerne. 'A week in lovely Lucerne' then cost £5 and a fortnight, I suppose, £8.

The middle classes rarely went abroad and up till then I had spent my holidays in such odd resorts as Lowestoft, Margate, Cromer, all considered by Victorians as bracing. One paddled in icy cold water and tried to shelter from the wind on sandy, crumbling cliffs behind tamarisk bushes. But by 1901 Cook's and the Polytechnic had succeeded in selling Switzerland to the public and my father.

The *pension* where we stayed in Lucerne was above the lake. A generous Swiss tourist agency provided us, for I should guess about 20 Swiss Francs, a fortnightly ticket allowing us to travel on all the railways, steamboats, funiculars, and other means of conveyance. With sandwiches provided by the *pension* this meant unlimited and uncostly excursions. But I at once felt an unreasonable dislike or indifference to Swiss mountains, lakes and *aussichtspunkte*, a dislike that persists.

No, looking back, perhaps there was a good reason. The *pension* was surrounded by a small garden, the intensely blue flowers of climbing morning glory mixed with the scarlet flowers of dustman's trumpet. There were low box hedges and I shall never forget the delicious acrid perfume of these plants in the hot sun. It will always be the essence of summer to me. When we went out into the garden after dinner there was an elderly lady sitting in a chair reading a book to a girl of about twenty. As hard as I try I cannot remember what she was like, if she was dark or fair, small or large. I only remember that she seemed to me to give out the same perfume as that hot summer garden and that she was the last of my pre-adolescent loves.

In some way or other I managed to get on speaking terms with this very reserved couple, so different from the other passing guests. One day the old lady spoke to me, perhaps because I always went about reading a book. She was a Russian countess and her ward a Spaniard from the Argentine. I never found out any more about them. I asked her if I might borrow the book she was reading, Daudet's *Sappho*.

"Vous êtes trop jeune, cher enfant, vous le lirez quand vous aurez vingt ans."

If I remember rightly Daudet dedicated his book to his son when he should reach twenty. Now it would not shock and still less amuse a child of twelve.

The result of this passion was that I lost all inclination to visit Swiss mountains, waterfalls or viewpoints and schemed to pass all my days in the hot little *pension* garden with the countess and her beautiful ward. I feigned headaches, tiredness, sickness to get out of the excursions and my mother, ever in favour of keeping the peace, helped me in my evasions, though I am sure she did not suspect the motive. I never declared my love. How could I? By what words or gestures? This seems to me the essence of childish love, that it demands no satisfaction or response; it is the love of the beautiful for itself, and the emotions felt are the same as those felt in looking at a picture, a landscape or hearing beautiful music.

We went back to London. On my thirteenth birthday I took part in a Jewish ceremony the name of which I have forgotten. You are called to read in a Synagogue a portion of the law. Afterwards there is a party and you are given presents. Amongst my presents were a number of gold sovereigns from my rich uncles. These I spent in buying the Elizabethan and Restoration dramatists in the Mermaid Series. Reading the plays and reading the notes I realised what England owed to Italy and determined that I must learn Italian and go to Italy.

My father had enjoyed his visit to Switzerland. There had been no bad smells, no immoral sights and no brigands to upset him. So next year we set out for Switzerland, for Ragaz on the way to the Engadine. This pleased me because I knew the inhabitants spoke *Romansch*, a dialect near to Italian. We were accompanied by my two maiden aunts and by my married aunt Sarah, whose husband was Dr Max Bernstein. Max was a Russian from Courland, where he had been court doctor to some local prince until an outburst of anti-semitism made him decide to settle in England. No one could have looked less conventionally Jewish than my uncle-in-law, with his very blue eyes, high cheek bones and a flat spreading nose. My uncle Max was not completely accepted in the family. He had many foreign habits such as taking tea with lemon and sucking it through a lump of sugar, and cracking the bones of chicken to extract the marrow, surely a sensible practice.

Well, here we were at Ragaz and a siren wind from Italy not so far away beckoned me. I entreated my father to go into Italy but he was adamant. Here I must explain the middle-class attitude at the beginning of the century to foreign countries. France was immoral and any Englishman going there ran grave moral risks. Italy was dangerous, immoral, dirty, diseased, and populated by brigands.

The safe countries were Switzerland, but better still was Germany, and there but for the grace of God and my own strong will I should have been educated. No one foresaw then, as no one foresees now after three terrible experiences, the German cruelty and lust for power, and what, for a young man, is worse – the lack of any innate sense of values, hidden and covered by a huge superstructure of learning.

I didn't go to Italy as I had hoped but my uncle suggested I should walk over the pass to Pontresina with him. I accepted with joy because Pontresina was an Italian name and nearer by some miles to the country I was longing to reach.

It was a comic expedition. The pass is not high but my uncle set out with almost as many trappings as the White Knight – a thermometer, an altimeter, several flasks, etc., and above all a large roll of brown paper. As the road got higher, he took down his trousers, exposing a broad behind, which he padded with successive rolls. As the road descended he stripped them off and arrived in Pontresina minus brown paper. That time I did not get to Italy.

I had a whole year before me in which I learnt a little Italian and read much about Italian art and literature. But most of all I worked on the feelings of my two aunts, who were fond of me as their only nephew, and my ever kind mother. Again we spent our holidays in Switzerland and they said they had been invited to meet some friends in Milan where there was an international exhibition and tickets at reduced rates.

Whether we met these friends or not I cannot remember, but we arrived at Venice at 5 a.m. as the dawn was breaking. They expected everything to be made of new and shining marble. I expected nothing. I can see the face they made when we got into a very decrepit gondola, rowed by an elderly shabby gondolier – instead of the handsome gondolier of the picture postcard. They looked with distaste at the ugly iron bridge and the ugly green copper dome of San Samuele, and the mouldering facades of the palaces, and with something more than distaste at the water rats scampering away from the gondola.

"Rats," they said. "There are rats everywhere where there is water and plenty in the Thames at Pangbourne where you live!"

They were terrified by the cries of the gondolier, *"stai"* and *"premi"*, as he turned to right or left. We had decided to go to the Hotel Commercio, an excellent old-fashioned Italian hotel, which we had chosen because it was not expensive. We arrived at the water entrance behind the Piazza and were received by a sleepy unshaved Italian wearing sloppy trousers and an open jacket showing a hairy chest, and out of nowhere sprang an old *gancino* anxious to earn a coin by hooking up a gondola.

"We can't stay here," my aunts said, "we must go to the best hotel."

I looked at my Baedeker and chose the Hotel Bauer-Grünwald, because it had a Germanic name, reassuring then to English ears. The price however was three times that of the Commercio. We took rooms but my aunts said: "Our rooms are three times as dear as those at the Commercio. We can only afford to stay here one day!" My aunts went to bed.

The sun had risen. I crossed the iron Accademia bridge, walked along the Zattere, somehow found my way to the Fondamento Nuovo and back to San Marco, without the aid of the ragamuffins who for a *soldo* would have guided me back to the Piazza. It was an hour of ecstasy.

I thought, "This is my town, this is my country. Am I perhaps a descendant of one of the Venetian Ghetto or of that converted Jew, Abarbanel Leone Hebreo, who was the priest of Aretino, Titian and other great men of the Renaissance?" At eleven o'clock I was back at the Bauer-Grünwald. My aunts were less frightened than they had been at 5 a.m. We got as far as Florian's and had an ice, but during the remaining few hours in Venice I could never persuade them to venture further than the first turning in the Merceria.

EROTIC LITERATURE, FOOD AND WINE

I returned from Paris last night, smuggling in my pockets the first two volumes of a very rare work in eleven volumes, *My Secret Life*. It is not in the British Museum. I do not know whether it is in the *Enfer de la Bibliothèque Nationale* or in the Vatican Library which naturally has the richest collection of pornography in the world.

For centuries the priest sitting in his confessional has had to consider and assess in terms of penance and absolution each sin of the flesh. They are the connoisseurs in such matters, and I know of no book more coldly obscene than the two volumes of Sanchez's *De Matrimonio*.

My Secret Life is a very rare book. Twenty copies only are supposed to have been printed and a recently published bibliography of erotic literature states that only one copy is known in a private collection. I could not help feeling the collector's thrill of pride at having acquired such a rarity.

It made me think of an earlier haul I made of erotic literature in Paris. Under the Third Empire there was a rich and socially ambitious merchant who had made the finest collection of such books in the world. By some means Napoleon learnt of the existence of this collection and expressed a wish to see it. One can imagine how flattered the aspiring merchant was to display it to his Emperor and what a pleasant evening they spent together, let us hope, over some bottles of pre-phylloxera claret. The next day Napoleon's police knocked at the door and seized the whole collection and it is now part of the *musée secret* of a great French library.

What Napoleon and his police did not remember was that the rich merchant had a château in the country where he kept an equally large collection of erotic books. This at least is the story which a Parisian bookseller told me round about 1939 and the story *se non è vero è ben trovato*, as the Italians say.

I was shown the remains of the collection which he had bought and what a collection it was! There were all the prettiest books of the eighteenth century with illustrations by Borel, there were the first editions of De Sade, the original edition of *Gamiani ou deux nuits d'excès*, said to have been written by Alfred de Musset after he broke with George Sand, illustrated by Daumier, and many more, all in sumptuous bindings. Besides the books, there was a great pile of erotic engravings.

How I sold the books is a story it would be indiscreet to tell. I sold them, but there still remained the prints and the problem of getting them back to England. At that time the customs were particularly severe. Joyce's *Ulysses* had been banned but every Englishman who went to Paris considered it his duty to bring home a copy. It is a clumsily shaped volume and the Customs easily detected it. I used to see piles of them on the customs bench at Dover. Once I asked an officer what was done with them. "Many a hearty laugh we all have over them between boats," was his reply. Legend has it that they were resold by the customs officers at fancy prices, but this no doubt is malicious gossip.

The books, as I say, were sold. There remained the problem of the prints. My wife came to the rescue. There are in my experience two classes of women, those who fear breaking the least letter of the law, and those who enjoy breaking the law just for the fun of doing it; those who tremble at the thought of smuggling half a nylon stocking, and those who would cheerfully try to smuggle fifty wrapped round a bar of gold or stuffed with uncustomed watches, just for fun!

My wife belonged to the latter class. So the prints came to England wrapped round her person. She looked as thought she was just on the point of giving birth to triplets. She was a fitting person for this enterprise, for her great uncle was Robert Samuel Turner, one of the famous bibliophiles of the nineteenth century. He died in 1887 and his superb collections were sold partly in Paris and partly in London, but a little time before his death he sold or gave the 'secret portion' of his collection to his friend Ashbee, who in turn left them to the British Museum, where they now repose in locked cases of which only the Keeper has the key.

Before I leave this subject, I would like to recall a very singular collector whose library consisted of books intended to illustrate the heights and depths of human nature. Beside the very rare first edition of the 'Imitation of Christ' you could find the equally rare first edition of De Sade's *Justine*; beside Spinoza's *Ethics* there stood the still rarer first edition of *Fanny Hill. Homo sum nihil humanum alicnum a me puto* must have been his motto.

To return to *My Secret Life*. I had always been curious about this book because of its extreme rarity and because the authorship had been attributed to a very distinguished Victorian statesman. A malicious friend suggests that it was by Gladstone. I read the first two volumes in the train. It is a very detailed account of the author's copulations from the age of puberty until about thirty, and the other nine volumes, which I have not read and shall not read probably, continue the story up to the author's old age. These memoirs are interesting perhaps for the picture they give of the sordidness of London life in the Victorian age, and of the way in which a gentleman then took his pleasure, but they lack atmosphere.

They do not ever evoke the 'ambiance' of the French brothels before they were closed by Madame Marthe Richard and of which I hope to write later. Lust without love or rather without fantasy is a dreary theme. It is the last erotic book which I shall read, unless in some papyrus are discovered the lost books of Elephantis. I shall subscribe to the first edition of them, read them and probably be disappointed. Why did the anonymous author write this book? To titillate his own or the reader's imagination? Why had the book left me so cold?

Reflecting on this theme, I returned to my flat in London with a basket of *morilles*, those delicious French mushrooms which grow in England but rot in the woods in which they grow. I opened that gastronomic bible Ali-Bab, to find how they should be cooked – *à la crème*, *au citron*, *au jus*, *en croustade*, *poulet aux morilles*, etc., etc. Tired as I was and heavy as the 1,280 page quarto volume of Ali-Bab is to hold, I read on until the early morning. I have read many erotic books and many cookery books and I asked myself why it is so much more amusing to read about the pleasures of the table than those of the bed. In the small hours of the morning, I resolved the problem, but as they are my reminiscences and not an attempt at psychoanalysis, I shall pass over the solution of the problem.

All this started in my mind a series of gastronomic reminiscences. I expect or hope I enjoyed my mother's milk or the substitute bottle, but cannot remember. The first real 'gastronomic' pleasure which I do remember is buying a liquorice strip for a penny or a halfpenny at a small shop at the corner of Quix Road on my way to my first Dame school. I doubt whether such sweets are manufactured now. It was a long pliable object which one tore into individual strips like black bootlaces and slowly sucked. Why the revolting flavour of liquorice should have been pleasing to a child's palate is a mystery!

In my family, food and still less wine were not considered seriously, although we probably ate better than most Englishmen do today. My father, who by the time I was twelve had developed some mysterious ailment, probably of nervous origin, never varied his diet for the 365 days of the year. At midday he ate a chop with greens, in the evening a steamed sole with rice pudding. My mother, as far as I remember, never went near the kitchen. She could no more have cooked a dish than she would have washed my father's shirts. 'As to cooking, our servants will do it for us,' to paraphrase Villiers de l'Isle Adam's words. That was her motto, and that of most ladies of the time.

At Cambridge, having been exempted from dining in hall by some wangle which I cannot recollect, I never varied my menu, cold mutton and mint sauce, which I ate alternately in my rooms and that of my friend Woolf in Trinity. My palate and my taste for food developed for the first time in Florence where Orioli and I established a bookshop in 1911. But we had little enough money to indulge our gastronomic tastes. A lira was what we spent on a meal, with a tip included. It was a good meal, pasta in all its varieties, meat and fruit and a *quartino* of wine, and if we were feeling rich we may have had another pennyworth of wine. But Orioli, like most Italians, was a good cook himself. He had seen his sisters cook and perhaps his father, and when at last we had a ménage of our own, Orioli did not disdain to go into the kitchen and cook the dishes of his native Romagna. Food became an interest for me and cooking, I gradually realised, the sixth art.

AUNTS AND UNCLES

I suppose most normal girls and boys are born not only with mothers and fathers, brothers and sisters but also with aunts and uncles. They stand in a different relationship to the child from their parents. Years have dimmed some of my memories. On my father's side I remember first of all my aunt Berinda. She was an unmarried lady, living by herself, and supported by my father. I think, but I am not sure, that she wore a wig. She was very deaf and conversation with her was not easy. I used to dread going to see her in the dreary little flat where she lived. The conversation was always the same, something like this: "You don't love your poor old aunt, do you! You are a naughty boy!" Protests from me in a childish voice which she probably did not hear. The only other remark which I ever remember her making was, "How many prizes have you won at school?" To which I could make no reply.

Then there was my aunt Esther, who lived in a large and gloomy house in Maida Vale. She had a big family, seven or eight children, including a daughter, with whom I was vaguely in love when I was fourteen, and a paralysed husband who had lain in bed for many years. I can recall then as now the horror of being taken to see him, to listen to his blurred speech and to smell the odour of sickness and decay which pervaded his room, and being asked to kiss his bearded face.

Aunt Rose. I have forgotten her other name, but her husband left her and had gone 'to the bad' as they say. She lived in a sordid flat in Gunnersbury. She had given birth to a freckled red-haired son who, I think, became a printer. But enough of my father's sisters.

Most vividly I recall my Uncle Alfred. Like my father he was a dentist, a handsome man who besides being a dentist was an artist who designed the scenery and costumes for several Alhambra ballets. At the age of forty-five the widow of a wine merchant living in one of those magnificent Victorian residences on Brixton Hill fell in love with him. She was over eighty. He married her *pour l'interêt* as the French say. With his wife's house and money he came into possession of the remains of a magnificent wine

104

cellar. Having been a teetotaller all his life, the vintage wines and spirits in his wife's cellars turned him into the classical Victorian and Edwardian drunkard.

In those days there were drunkards in the land. Some of my early childhood recollections are of a policeman knocking at the door and of my father being called to bail out Uncle Alfred who had been arrested for drunkenness. On the rare occasions when he visited our house, sober of course, he delighted my sister and myself by his conjuring tricks. The poor man expected and hoped that his wife would have died before he did, as logically she should have, but in fact he 'drank himself to death' – which was a Victorian habit – and she survived him and I think died at the age of ninety-five.

My aunts. Aunt Sarah taught me to read. The earliest work I can ever remember reading or having read to me is an article in a popular encyclopaedia on bees. I have always loved bees and perhaps my later enthusiasm for these insects, whose way of life I now disapprove of, was inspired by my early readings.

Aunt Sarah was my favourite aunt. Small, dark and I should now say ugly, she had a beautiful voice, a feeling for music and had sung in the Carl Rosa Opera Company. I hated however seeing her sing – with that opening of the mouth which suggests a visit to the dentist or a preparation for a gargle.

She married a Russian doctor from Lithuania, Max Bernstein, who, I believe, was unfaithful to her and who, by the bye, was the first person who tried to tell me the 'facts of life', and said that if I wanted to make love I should choose 'a nice clean girl' without telling me how to do so.

Aunt Rhoda. I can remember very little about her except that she was beautiful. She married a Levantine Jew from Smyrna, David Sidi, fascinating now to me in recollection because his native language was Spanish, the Castilian of the sixteenth century spoken by the exiled Spanish Jews who – as it is said – still have the keys of their houses in Toledo – waiting to return. He was, nevertheless, the ruin of my own and my sister's hopes of fortune because, from my father, he borrowed the legacy left us by my grandmother in a vain attempt to corner the market in Smyrna figs. The fortunes of this family sunk lower and lower and I shall not try to trace them.

Uncles. Uncle Nat. A glorious figure, in his prime resembling Edward VII, always immaculately dressed, always smelling of eau-de-Cologne and always, when I went to see him at my grandmother's house on Sunday morning – at eleven o'clock because he rose late – taking out from his sovereign case one or more golden coins. Unfortunately, like most of my family, he came to a sad end.

My grandmother, whom I knew, was the wife of an incompetent 'dreamer of the ghetto', a pious student of the Talmud, whom I never knew. He died, I think, before I was born. My grandmother had a business head and established a mantle factory in the City to which she was driven every day from her house, Cromer Lodge, in West End Lane, in a four-wheeled cab.

But unfortunately there came a moment when mantles were no longer fashionable. This took a long time for my grandmother and her sons to realise, and they kept on manufacturing mantles and hoping that one day they would again be wanted. By the time my grandmother was dead, by the time my uncle had squandered the family fortune in living in the grand Edwardian style, the business was bankrupt.

I can still see my unfortunate uncle, the ghost of his former self, creeping into my shop in Museum Street, on his way to try to find something to do in the City. Meanwhile, before his downfall, he had married a glamourous chorus girl. It was the thing to do in those days and my uncle had followed the Edwardian tradition. His son was Rodney Acland.

Uncle Frank. He was the younger brother of Uncle Nat. My recollections of him are dimmer. I only remember when I was probably about twelve being invited to his future bride's house in Bayswater, and at the end of the luncheon having set before me a finger bowl which I drank because I did not know what else to do with it.

THE MAGIC CHEST
I have always thought that in the course of one's life, one should experience everything, the heights and the depths. Even in my business career as a dealer in rare books I am glad to have known moments when I did not know how to pay my creditors, when my bank manager ominously asked me to call on him and I, with a sinking feeling in the pit of my stomach, was interviewed by him in his office.

Of course there have happily been other times when I have been on the crest of the wave of fortune. Luckily in the life of a bookseller there are these ups and downs, so that to employ a cliché, there is never a dull moment. I am therefore glad in retrospect to have been once in my life thoroughly swindled by an artist in this line. If she has now been released from prison, I hope she will pay me a visit, so that I may congratulate her. I think she could easily persuade me to part with another few hundred pounds.

About five years ago a friendly but cautious exiled German bookseller asked me whether I would care to see a lady who claimed that she owned some books and autography of immense value, adding that if I came to terms with her, he would expect a percentage! So Frau … turned up in my office in Maddox Street. She was a middle-aged German Frau, shabbily dressed, wearing a worn out Macintosh because, she said, she had been obliged to sell her furs. She was the widow, she said, of a Czech general.
....

JUVENILIA AND *JUNIORA*
These recollections are neither for eventual publication, broadcasting or any other form of publicity but for myself and the few friends who might be interested. Nor are they for the psychoanalyst whom so far I have avoided.

Nothing is more false than to ignore, ridicule, or minimise the loves of one's youth. I suppose I loved my mother and hated my father in the classical pattern. I can't remember having done so. But my earliest recollections of love is having fallen in love at the probable age of seven with a friend of my sister's called Madge Goldring, and it surprises me with my failing memory that I can remember her name. Beyond her name I can remember nothing except climbing into her bed and I suppose cuddling her. I wonder what she has become!

My next love recollection is when I was about ten I suppose and was taken to the chilly seaside town, Lowestoft, which was in those days considered 'bracing'. There, how I don't know, I met a to me enchanting girl whose name I have forgotten. I wish I hadn't. We used to meet in a cave under the cliffs and exchange passionate kisses, nothing else, but even now at the distance of sixty years I can still imagine those kisses and think that I have never enjoyed kisses so much. Who was she? Shall I ever know?

And then there was another girl, a daughter of a friend of my aunts, who I loved equally passionately but I can't think of her name. Again we used to meet and kiss passionately.

I would love to know what has happened to her. Almost certainly dead I suppose. I would like to put an advertisement in the agony columns of *The Times* – 'Wanted to meet lady who, in around about 1899–1900, was embraced and loved by Irving Davis', but I shall not.

Of course, lying back as it were on the psychoanalyst's couch – but really sitting at the kitchen table – I can think of many more passionate youthful loves, but I think these are enough.

I was not born a homosexual. I can't remember ever feeling in love with a boy until my Cambridge days and later, my Florence days, when homosexuality was almost compulsory, but that will be another chapter of this my imagined autobiography as will my early sexual experience.

Note by Patience Gray: Irving gave me this fragment to type in April 1966 as a 'first draft'… he was not able to complete the memoirs. I reproduced the typescript for 'the few friends who might be interested' in Britain, France, Italy and Catalonia; it was received with pleasure and delight. With the approval of Irving's step-daughter Ianthe Carswell, not wishing to deprive readers of these recollections, fascinating in themselves, Tom Jaine and I decided to transgress Irving's instructions, stated in the first sentence of JUVENILIA AND JUNIORA, and put them into print.

L'Amico Nostro

Irving told me his dreams, which is how my belief was confirmed that his was the soul of a White She-Cat.

An Irving dream: "I was sitting in the Underground, the tube train hurtling to Camden Town in the middle of the night. I was surprised to find that the person sitting beside me in an otherwise empty compartment was Oscar Wilde. We were talking as old friends. Suddenly the train stopped. A white cat leapt out. I tried to follow it but it disappeared in a labyrinth of tunnelled corridors."

When the time drew close for dying he often said: "What is going to happen to *my cats*? They must be put to sleep." This, in a particular voice, which conveyed that he was talking about himself, the same small high voice he used in talking to cats.

Sometime before that Irving's white cat Lesbia, neurotic creature, after a protracted diet of grouse, pheasant, prawns and pâté, not improbably developed a cankerous malady. It was relegated to a 'good home' in the country to which it was driven by Ianthe in a closed car. It never reached this destination. At some traffic lights in the East End – they were heading for Essex – the cat leapt dexterously out of the car – how could it when the car was closed? – threaded its way through three lines of arrested motor cars and vanished for ever. This happening represented for me that Irving's soul was free.

In Carrara where men lived an unspeakably long time I often see an old man's backview poised on the curb – resolute but hesitant – which reminds me of Irving. *Il Professore* (more accurately *il Commendatore*) seems to be advancing in front of me, head forward, nose in the air, shoulders bent, hands clasped on an extinct Toscana behind his back, wisps of grey hair tickling the collar of a blue cotton ensemble, his ancient 'summer uniform', up how many Italian streets – in Positano, Agropoli, Firenze, Roma, Napoli, Venezia, Lecce, Taranto.

I see him too havering up Cannon Lane in late November after lunch in a high wind in beret and old coat, dangling a transparent bag which had contained the claret, as light, as frail as a windblown leaf.

But why his Backview?

It is impossible to have such a thing as a Front View of Irving. The first time we met he shook my hand while glancing determinedly away, beside, beyond me. How many times subsequently I saw him meet others in this way. His oblique glance repudiated the direct encounter. (On reflection, I realise that all his relationships were oblique, triangulated.) I recognised this glance again in Bernini's Elephant in the *piazza della Rotonda* in Rome, and once took a photograph of these kindred spirits when we stayed in the Albergo Minerva, then only frequented by priests. We stayed there – a rather gloomy place – in order to feed the thousand cats lurking in the Pantheon ditch.

The gourmet aspect of Irving has been underlined; from all accounts he must have been sitting at table for almost half a century. But how often has he in fact ordered a *palomba* or delicate red mullet in order it appeared to deposit most of it in a paper bag at the corner of some Venetian *calle* at a midnight rendezvous with already waiting cats. And it wasn't for the *frutte di mare* that we went to Taranto one summer. It was because it was said by the Ancients *and* Norman Douglas to be the place where The Cat was first introduced from Egypt.

I became a student of the Oblique Approach only when I met Irving in the 1950s. His words guarded rather than illuminated his thoughts, but both were essentially vehicles for feelings. The themes recurred. "Yes, let me see, what *did* we eat last night?" There followed a Precise Catalogue, and then the Judgement, seldom complimentary unless he had just flown back from Paris. Another, more dramatic: "I suppose I've already told you, I'm *ruined*!" (iniquities of the Income Tax; a valuable book has disappeared; a Marquis in Florence fails to keep his word). Another theme, a perfect goldmine: The horrors, errors, plagiarisms committed by the Writers of Cookery Books.

There were other themes: "I swear I shall never set foot in Spain again as long as Franco is alive." (Rash vow, often broken, since two of his Catalan friends, Fenosa and Nicole spent half the year there.) And then: "Do you realise what an awful place England is?" This usually led to a revelation of the crimes perpetrated by English green-grocers, butchers, fishmongers, but was equally sparked off by journalistic illiteracy, false attributions and political ineptitude.

These Hobbyhorses, spurred on by an excellent claret poured into Venetian glasses while some delicious dish was simmering, were mounted in the New End kitchen, and provided they were given their head were eventually laid aside for more enthralling disquisitions on the richly coruscated past or tracts from Irving's personal Utopia which lay somewhere in the future. They were an evening exercise, preliminary skirmishes to determine precisely how or what he was felling at that moment. I was delighted by these flights of egotism. His epistolary diatribes had an equally exhilarating effect. They also explain why Irving's friends were almost always women. He was a perfect cure for self-preoccupation. There was no question of competing. If this arose, Irving simply didn't listen.

In a cloud of cigar smoke I swing back to Irving's dream: "I was walking along a country road; in the distance I discerned a horse and cart drawn up on the roadside. Getting nearer, I saw it was a rag-and-boneman's cart. It was stacked high with books. I looked at the books, they were absolutely *priceless*. The rag-and-boneman let me have the lot for sixpence!" (This dream recurred.)

Here is the traumatic source of Irving's fantastic optimism; he was in nocturnal touch with the Miraculous. He was however equally accessible to Despair, of which the Rubbish Heap was its most haunting symbol. He was all hopes, fears, dreads, loves, wishes, feelings – daily in expectation of a disaster or a miracle. Meanwhile he acquired books like experts acquire cheeses, by smell, feel, touch, I have often seen him. (He was always flopping cigar ash over the open pages of priceless books, and let one handle the most marvellous illustrated manuscripts without a second thought.)

I am supposed to be writing about Irving as a cook. There is not much to say except I learned anything I know from him. He was always rather shocked that I had had the Temerity to write a cookery book *before I knew him*. I came more and more to understand that. And it was perhaps why after our first encounter at the Carswells he invited me very soon to Brunswick Square to dinner. It was a *Canard à l'orange*. "My cooking days are over," he remarked in front of this perfectly classical and tangible testimony to the contrary.

Irving's sense of perfection found complete expression in his cooking. Can I say more than that. This had in the remoter past led to his flinging a to him imperfect creation, another duck, out of the window in the presence of several expectant guests, – which creature got unexpectedly hitched onto a drainpipe several storeys up and had eventually to be rescued by a fire engine on account of neighbourly complaints – it being high summer at the time.

At Irving's table I learned the full poetic meaning of the word 'classical', in which all forethought, selection, trouble, timing (the mechanics of creation) were erased by the disarming simplicity of the outcome, which gave rise only to pleasure and delight. It was here that was reflected that diametrically opposite conjunction of *liberality* and *frugality* which characterized Irving's way of life, and which incidentally is the masterkey to the culinary art. Irving's dishes were an invocation to the ideal; his method of presenting them celebrated his Mediterranean past. The result was a kind of alchemy by which the past was here made present; it made me feel in knowing him I held the key to that lost Bohemia where Boris Koutzoff, Orioli, Douglas, Ivy, Lawrence, Firbank, Beerbohm were creatures of substance, not of reminiscence.

Those *were* memorable meals. I am not going to list them. It was at these feasts that Irving first rehearsed his Memoirs. His gift for writing, his mastery of understatement was completely thwarted by his conversational powers. Someone once laid the accusation of frivolity at Irving's door; I think with him all other considerations were overridden in favour of delighting a very few people in the moment now. When I realise that one evening the whole preposterous Episode of the Magic Chest was recounted to me (an opening fragment of which appears in the Memoirs) and that I have forgotten it in every hallucinating detail, I beat my breast.

To those who loved Irving these recollections are bound to be inadequate; each must cherish his own *souvenirs*. He always claimed that he knew Only Five People – perfectly untrue – and swore he was incapable of recalling or recognising anyone else. Even by the oblique system of triangulation these five people must at least be doubled